CAMBRIDGESHIRE FOLK TALES

T0347574

CAMBRIDGESHIRE
FOLK
TALES

MAUREEN JAMES

The History Press

*For all the Fen Tigers, who I hope will appreciate and enjoy this book.
And to Aunty Joan and Uncle Tom, whose love
and inspiration stay with me always.*

First published 2014
Reprinted 2023

The History Press
97 St George's Place,
Cheltenham, Gloucestershire, GL50 3QB
www.thehistorypress.co.uk

British Library Cataloguing in Publication Data.
A catalogue record for this book is available from the British Library.

ISBN 978 0 7524 6628 6

Typesetting and origination by The History Press
Printed by TJ Books Limited, Padstow, Cornwall

CONTENTS

ACKNOWLEDGEMENTS

This book follows on from my other volume in the same series, namely *Lincolnshire Folk Tales*. For both I have drawn on research carried out on the folklore and folk tales of the flatlands for my PhD. However, it would not have been possible without the initial inspirations provided by Barbara Johnson and Heather Falvey that revived my passion for history back in 1985. I am also indebted to Liz Wright for persuading me that I could write professionally, Paul Jackson for showing me the power of the spoken story, and Del Reid for being a tower of strength for so many storytellers. I also would like to thank the late Doug Stone of Chatteris and Peter Hewitt of March, for sharing not just with me, but with many, many others, their love of local history. Similarly, I owe a debt of gratitude to the folklorists of the past, especially Enid Porter and the late W.H. Barrett (and his informants). Numerous other storytellers and historians have also inspired me on my journey, but with regards to Cambridgeshire and the Fens, these include Hugh Lupton, Malcolm Busby, Polly Howat, Mike Petty, Celia and Geoff Taylor, Judith Legge, Gordon Phillips, Nicky Stockman, Alan Lamb, Ernie Hall and the late Arthur Dunham. Finally, I need to thank my husband Stuart for helping with the illustrations, and he and the rest of my family for their patience and understanding.

> *Maiden's garter, fenman's charter,*
> *Neighbours brats, fishermans floats,*
> *fire a' glowing, reaper mowing,*
> *are things never interfered with.*

Map of
Cambridgeshire

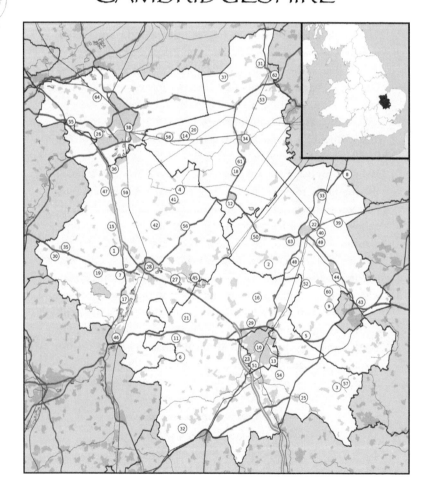

Places Included in this Book

INTRODUCTION

*On its borders Hickathrifts castle once stood, and in its mazes
Hereward sought shelter during his long struggle for independence.*

Jonathan Peckover, 1868

Like the other books within this History Press series, this volume
is a collection of folk tales linked to the landscape and to a specific
county. The county in this case is Cambridgeshire, formed in 1965
by the joining of the historic county of Cambridgeshire with the
Isle of Ely and, in 1974, with the addition of Huntingdonshire and
the Soke of Peterborough (part of the unitary authority).

THE LANDSCAPE: THEN AND NOW

The present county of Cambridgeshire is bordered on the north
by Lincolnshire, on the east by Norfolk and Suffolk, on the south
by Essex and Hertfordshire and on the west by Bedfordshire and
Northamptonshire.

A glance at an Ordnance Survey map will show that much of the
northern part of the county consists mostly of very low-lying land,
the silt and peat fenland, interspersed with similarly low-lying islands.

Daniel Defoe, in his *Tour Through the Eastern Counties of
England* (1722), noted that the Fens were the 'sink of no less than

thirteen counties' being subject regularly to inundation by the rivers 'Cam or Grant, the Great Ouse and Little Ouse, the Nene, the Welland, and the Lark'.

The situation is still the same today, and the area still carries the run-off water from Bedfordshire, Buckinghamshire, Cambridgeshire, Essex, Huntingdonshire, Leicestershire, Lincolnshire, Norfolk, Northamptonshire, Oxfordshire, Rutland, Suffolk and Warwickshire. However, there is now an elaborate system of moving the flood waters out to the Wash.

With the shrinkage of the peat, almost all of the Fenland rivers are now above the level of the land, some many feet higher, making a strange sight with the river banks rising high above the roads that run beside them. There are also numerous drainage dykes crossing the Fens, into which the Fenland waters are pumped on their way to the sea. It has been estimated that when all the pumping stations in the Fens are busy they can move a total of ten million gallons of water per minute.

But what of the landscape before all the pumps and drains?

In 1868 Jonathan Peckover of Wisbech described the county before the extensive drainage of the seventeenth century:

> the inland water extended as far south as Cambridge, and touched on the east, Downham, Brandon and Mildenhall; Soham being upon a lengthy neck of land which stretched out into the morass. On the west side were St Ives, Somersham, Ramsey, Peterborough and Peakirk. The sea entered at three outlets from the north, the widest of which passed by Wisbech, another at Spalding and a third at Lynn, the sea coast from Lynn running northward and passing a short distance from Castle Rising. There was thus between Wisbech and Lynn, a large oblong island of 'marshland', upon the upper part of which was Walpole, and on the lower side Hickathrifts castle at Emneth ... There was also another larger island called Holland between Wisbech and Spalding, which with the one just mentioned formed the northern border of the great inland swamp of waters called the Fens. Upon the southern borders of Holland were Crowland and Guyhirn. In the

waters of the Fens were scattered a great number of islands, upon some of the principal of which were situated Thorney, Whittlesey, March, Chatteris and Littleport. The largest island was a straggling piece of ground which was called the Isle of Ely, near the north of which was Ely and the south, Haddenham.

This low-lying land, despite the regular winter flooding was not uninhabited. The silt fens in the northern part of the county, a remnant of the ancient and frequent inundations of the sea, were once the least populated. The fertile band of sandy, brownish-grey soil that stretches from Holland in Lincolnshire in the north and west, to the Norfolk marshlands in the east, with its southern boundary following a line from Littleport to Thorney via Guyhirn, was later to prove ideal for the planting of apple orchards, which were once a major feature of the area.

Further south, on the islands and fen edges, the people were engaged in agriculture, whilst in the areas of bog, marsh and fen, the inhabitants lived off the abundant fish and fowl. Many of the former islands can be recognised by the names that end in the Saxon 'ea' or 'ey' such as Manea, Thorney and Ramsey, meaning island.

A medieval description records that around the Isle of Ely:

> In the eddies at the sluices … are netted innumerable eels, large water-wolves, with pickerels, perches, roaches, burbots, and lampreys … It is indeed said by many that sometimes salmon are taken there, together with the royal fish, the sturgeon … There you find geese, teal, coot, didappers, water-crows, herons and ducks, more than man can number, especially in winter or at moulting time. I have seen a hundred — nay, even three hundred — taken at once; sometimes by bird-lime, sometimes in nets or snares.

It is the eels that were most profitable, and they became almost a currency, and were used to pay tithes. It has been calculated that in the twelfth century the villages of Littleport, Stuntney and Doddington contributed 68,000 eels to the Abbot of Ely.

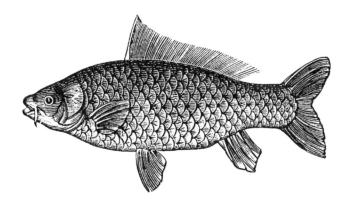

In the seventeenth century the whole of the landscape of this Great Level began to be transformed, as drainage turned it into a vast plane, intersected by a huge network of drainage ditches, 'dykes' or 'lodes' of various sizes, but all interconnected and all involved in carrying excess water to be pumped out to the sea.

But in the seventeenth century, successful campaigns resulted in permission to drain the whole area, to stop the flooding and to turn the land over to year-round pasture or agricultural land.

The 750,000 acres became known as the Bedford Level after the Earl of Bedford, who led the team of fourteen adventurers who invested in the undertaking. In return for their investment, carried out under the instructions of the Dutch drainage engineer Cornelius Vermuyden, the gentlemen were granted ownership of the drained land. For administrative purposes the fen was divided into three parts, the North Level, South Level and Middle Level.

Not everyone supported the drainage, which changed the wetland to rich brownish-black peaty fenland soil. There were riots in a number of places, including Whelpmore Fen in 1638 when a crowd, supposedly playing football, levelled the ditches. 'Fen football', in which the residents of two or more villages would meet at some open-air spot, was one of the more common means of attacking both drainage works and enclosures.

Other methods were also used by these 'Fen Tigers' including threats to workmen, masked attacks and direct sabotage. In 1641 a boat packed with burning hassocks (bundles of straw) was directed down a channel into Littleport sluice gate.

And so, despite the opposition, the peat bogs, silt fens and marshes were drained, with varying degrees of success, and the people were enabled not only just to grow useful crops, but also to raise cattle and sheep on summer pastures. The place names indicate some of the former uses, such as the Fodder, Mow, Turf and Sedge Fens and the woodland terms such as *stocking* and *hurst*.

The initial drainage of the Fens only took the water down to a certain level and, as a consequence, a number of deep lakes, or meres, were left. These included Whittlesey Mere, Ramsey Mere, Benwick Mere, Ugg Mere and Trundle Mere, all of which remained until the nineteenth century when pumping engines enabled them to be drained. By 1850, Whittlesey Mere was so shallow as to be no longer navigable and it was emptied as a private enterprise to change over 3,000 acres of peat-covered swamp into rich agricultural land.

It was not until the nineteenth century, and the introduction of steam-powered pumps, that the land could be kept reliably drained all year round – and for decades this land has provided rich flat farmland. Today, the Great Level, though relatively treeless, has its own kind of beauty, with extended views, magnificent sunsets and 'big' skies. The straight-edged fields are extensive and the soil – fine black peat virtually free from stones – enables the growing of crops in abundant harvests, particularly sugar beet, root vegetables and potatoes.

With regards to the rest of the county, low chalk uplands extend over much of the southern half, and include the East Anglian Heights. This chalk ridge straddles England from the Yorkshire coast, across the Home Counties and down to the coast of Devon. The mean height of this range is 400–500 feet. However, in Cambridgeshire, the highest point is at Great Chishill (at just under 480 feet).

And now, before we move on, I would like to say a few words about the former administrative districts:

The Old Shire of Cambridge

The old county of Cambridgeshire was formed at the junction of the old kingdoms of Mercia and East Anglia, with the rivers Cam and Ouse providing the natural boundary markers. The rivers Cam and Granta and their various tributaries have eroded broad valleys out of the low chalky uplands of the shire. The Cam, also called the Rhee, has its source in the springs that can be found across the county boundary at Ashwell, Hertfordshire. The Granta rises similarly near Saffron Walden, Essex.

The Old Shire of Huntingdon

The old county (now district) of Huntingdonshire lies in the west of Cambridgeshire and, as such, contains in the south and west many hills and valleys, none of which are particularly deep but each containing a stream that flows into the Ouse or the Nene rivers. Both rivers rise in Northamptonshire and make their way leisurely to the sea at the Wash. In the north and east of old Huntingdonshire lies a level plain of fenland; indeed the lowest physical point in the UK, namely Holme Fen at 9ft below sea level, is within this district.

The Isle of Ely

The former administrative area that includes the island on which the city of Ely is situated was once under the jurisdiction of the Bishops of Ely. Formerly an impenetrable waste of reedy meres and trackless bogs, for it is well below sea level, the area was interspersed with islands, the largest of which contained the cathedral, affectionately known as the 'Ship of the Fens', as it is clearly visible from many miles away and seems to float over the landscape.

The Soke of Peterborough

The historic region surrounding the town of Peterborough was known as the Soke, or the Liberty, of Peterborough, as it used to be under the jurisdiction of the abbot of the monastery and independent of lay authority. The Soke has been part of the county of

Northamptonshire but is now a unitary authority. In view of its position, I have included it within this book.

BUT WHAT OF THE PEOPLE WHO TOLD THESE STORIES IN THE PAST, AND THE PEOPLE WHO COLLECTED THEM?

In the days before the invention of modern lighting, and when the working day was dependent on the availability of natural light or candlelight, life was much different to today. Long winter evenings meant that people gathered together, talked, sang, played music and told stories to each other.

Before the introduction of compulsory education, lessons would be taught, reminiscences shared and news would also be spread by word of mouth. As the historian Ekirch noted, 'legends, fables and tales of evils spirits, eternal stories recounted again and again by seasoned narrators with well trained memories' filled the time, and whilst the people gathered around the fire, they would carry out indoor tasks such as knitting, weaving, carding wool and basket making.

But perhaps one of the most popular places for the telling of tales was in the public houses, such as The Ship at Brandon Creek. This pub played host, particularly on Saturday nights, to a number of wonderful storytellers who entertained the young **Walter Henry Barrett** (1891–1974) who would sit quietly in the corner with his friend, the landlord's son. Nicknamed 'Jack' because when he was young he resembled an uncle by that name, Barrett eventually had to stop his weekly visits to The Ship, when his father, a lay preacher 'inflicted such punishment' on him that he realised that if he continued with his pursuit of learning about the past of Fenland and old Fen Lore it was 'going to be a painful one'.

But Barrett could not easily forget the tales he had heard from those old men, who he described as 'past masters in the art of storytelling'. He also saw each of the old men as 'a storehouse of folklore stories, many of which had been handed down from generation to generation, told and retold in the days when listeners sat enthralled by what was, more or less, their only means of recreation'.

In later life, Barrett was prompted by Alan Bloom, author of several books on the Fens, to write down on paper the stories he recalled. Bloom suggested that the Cambridge Folk Museum contact Barrett and, as a result of this, Enid Porter established a friendship with Barrett and included some of his recollections in *Cambridgeshire Customs and Folklore*. The stories were also edited as *Tales from the Fens* and *More Tales From the Fens*. Barrett also recalled a number of tall tales, and a visit to the Fens by Mark Twain, which are included in this book.

Arthur Randell (1901–88) similarly recalled many humorous stories. Brought up in the village of Magadalen, Norfolk, near Wisbech and by the River Great Ouse, he spent much of his working life as a signalman at Waldersea siding, and on retirement he returned to his father's profession of mole catching, covering 4,000 acres of the Fens. His memories of Fen people, their beliefs, lives and ways were edited by Enid Porter and recorded in the books *Sixty years a Fenman* (1966) and *Fenland Memories* (1969). Randell, who told Polly Howat that she 'shouldn't believe everything he told her', noted that:

> Like a good many others Fen people can tell some very 'tall' tales when they like; they look on them as a good joke and don't really expect them to be believed. Perhaps it is round the taproom fire in some pub on a winter's evening that such stories are most often heard, the tellers good-naturedly trying to out-do one another in relating the most outlandish yarns they know, all the time swearing that what they say is 'Gospel truth'. I remember, as a young man, being one day in the company of three old Magdalen people, two men and a woman, and the talk got round to the strong winds we had been having recently. One of the old chaps said they were nothing to those he remembered as a boy when there had been such a gale blowing over the Fens one day that when twilight came the crows had to walk home.

Enid Porter (1909–84) found that the telling of tall tales was frequently rewarded within the county:

> It was customary to reward the narrators [of tales] with some token of the listeners' appreciation. The award usually took the form of free beer, but there were other prizes – a 'silver' cup … a ribbon rosette, or a medal. These were usually kept in the public house and solemnly handed to the teller of the story which was judged to be the 'tallest' of the evening.

In the Cambridge Museum there is a rudely crafted, iron 'medal' bearing the words 'THE NOTED LIAR'. Found in the garden of The Pike and Eel pub at Chesterton, near Cambridge, the 1.5-inch diameter disc is likely to have been a medal given to a good storyteller. Porter noted that the inn was a popular meeting place of not just local people, but also watermen on the lighters and barges that carried goods between the city and King's Lynn.

One of the storytellers who inspired Barrett, and whose tales are not just included in his books but also inspired some within this volume, is **William 'Chafer' Legge** (1838–1909). One of ten children born to William Legge, a carpenter and wheelwright in Southery, Chafer never learnt to read and write but knew all about fishing and fowling, which supplemented his income as an agricultural labourer. In his younger days, Chafer also gained a reputation as a skater and bare-fist fighter. When he was 21 he married Susan Porter and they lived in a small wooden shack on the Fens. Chafer was described as a striking character wearing an otterskin cape, moleskin trousers and waistcoat. He and his wife had eight children, a number of whom were also good skaters. Barrett described how Chafer's daughter Susan was taking part in the women's skating championships as the 'favourite': 'Suddenly she began to slow down. Some of her undies were slipping. Her father seeing what was happening and having a lot of money on his daughter, cupped his hands to his mouth and shouted, "Keep going Susan, you never wore none till you went to service." A kick and a shake and Susan won.'

James Wentworth Day (1899–1983), another writer and collector of stories, who inspired a number of the tales within this book, is of a completely different social class from Legge. Born at Exning, Suffolk, Day was a writer and broadcaster, firmly of the Agrarian Right school and essentially a High Tory, who at one time owned Adventurers' Fen, a piece of marshland in Cambridgeshire. Day was closely associated with the *East Anglian Magazine* and was editor of *East Anglia Life* from 1962 until 1966. However, as is noted later in this book, it appears that Day 'never let the truth get in the way of a good story'.

Of the stories from Huntingdonshire, one of the main sources is **W.H. Bernard Saunders** (1839–1913). Saunders was not just the compiler of *Legends and Traditions of Huntingdonshire* but also the editor of *Fenland Notes & Queries* from 1891 to 1897. Yet at the time of writing, despite much searching, I have been unable to find out any more about Saunders.

Arthur Dunham, who died in 2013 at the age of 84, provided the substance of at least two of the tall stories. A tall, lanky fen farmer, he and his wife Margaret attended a number of meetings of the Fenland-based storytelling group Fables, Tales and Folklore, where Arthur generously shared his stories. Arthur and his wife also planted their own broadleaved woodland between 1985 and 1991. Known as Dunham's Wood it was open to the public on a number of weekends each summer, and was a wonderful attraction for families for many years. Sadly, the wood – which is two miles east of March, just off the March to Downham Market road (B1099) – is now closed to the public.

I have also referred to some storytellers who are still practising the art today, one of the most notable of whom is **Polly Howat**. A published author of six books of folklore and legends, Howat has also released an audio tape of *Tales from the Misty Fen*. She has been a professional storyteller for many years and in 1979 she led an oral history project in the Cambridgeshire, West Norfolk and Lincolnshire Fens.

Another inspiration is **Alan Lamb**, a very unassuming gentleman from Farcet who regularly entertains local groups with mostly humorous tales from the Fens, some true and some not so …

Similarly **Malcolm Busby**, one of the Cambridge Storytellers, has been telling many local stories to community groups for many years and, whilst doing so, has been given a few more for his repertoire!

It is interesting to note from local informants that there were other local people (aside from those who Barrett listened to at Brandon Creek) who were known as good storytellers. One was the elderly landlord of The Fisherman's Rest at Purl's Bridge, Manea, who entertained his customers about fifty years ago; another was the Great Eastern Railway guard who spent his childhood in Cambridgeshire, and who told the Two Fat Geese story to Mr Paddick from Hoddesdon (included in Chapter 3). Malcolm Busby also recently met a woman in Orton Waterville whose grandfather, Frank Jeeves, was a former soldier who used to tell stories in pubs in Peterborough and south Lincolnshire, in exchange for beer.

However, generally across the county (and elsewhere), as literacy took hold people began to regard the traditional popular pastimes, particularly storytelling, as belonging to a different world to their own. The school inspectors, schoolmasters and the clergy who preached in the pulpits and ran the Sunday schools openly discouraged superstitious beliefs.

As L.F. Newman, the Cambridge-based president of the short-lived Eastern Counties Folklore Society noted:

> Only tantalising fragments … [of stories, beliefs and customs] … have survived and from them the folklorist has to build up the main structure of his science. The spread of education led to a wilful and deliberate attempt to stamp out the old rural culture …

Thankfully, people like those mentioned above recognised that these influences were in danger of resulting in the loss of an important part of the cultural history of this land and they diligently recorded (and also transformed or even suppressed) the old stories 'according to personal tastes and circumstances'.

However, as these collectors of folklore and stories carried out their important work, the competition from books and newspapers that provided informative accounts of current affairs began to be viewed in many places as more important than listening to the old storytellers. Such entertainment was considered only to be suitable for the very young, or very old, but at what loss?

In 1934 John Beverley Nichols noted in his *Book of Old Ballads*, that 'the mysteries have gone. We know … what lies on the other side of the hill. The scientists have long ago puffed out, scornfully, the golden lamp of the night … leaving us in the utmost darkness.'

We are very fortunate that the stories of Cambridge were preserved, mostly in print, but some in the oral tradition, so that we can continue to hear them. Within this county a small group of friends from the Ouse Washes Molly Dancers have also been spreading the tales, as part of a number of major schools projects. Their latest, the Enid Porter Project, is also increasing awareness of the county folklore collection. I hope that this book will complement such initiatives.

About This Book

I am very grateful to The History Press for assisting in the rekindling of interest in the art of oral storytelling. They purposefully chose people who actually tell stories (rather than read them) and who live in, or have a deep interest in, their respective counties to be the authors.

I have aimed within this volume to provide a mix of stories that I tell, stories I have heard, stories in their original form and stories that contain a mix of all of these. I would also like to add that I should not be given all the credit for passing on these tales. I would like to acknowledge the tellers of the past and the people who told the stories to them, in an unbroken chain back to the original observer or creator of the tale.

I have tried, where possible, to acknowledge the individual tellers or recorders of the folk tales, where such information is available, and have also included historical notes, some location details and other snippets of relevant information or summaries of similar, or related tales. All these, I hope, will help the future tellers, or readers of the stories, to put the narratives into context and within the Cambridgeshire landscape.

I have arranged the tales into seven chapters – Of the Fens and Farming; Of Strange Phenomena; Of Rumour, Gossip and Tall Stories; Of Witchcraft and Murder; Of People and Places; Of Churches, Parsons and Saints, and Of Kings and Castles. At the end of the book I have also included a list of the sources consulted.

Fur, feather and fish piled up on a dish,
A man in a boat without a coat,
a bitch of a witch and a winding ditch,
And flickering lights are some of the sights
one sees when down in the fen.

1

OF THE FENS AND FARMING

In this section I have included a number of tales connected to the rural landscape and the plight of people living within such an environment. The first concerns the legendary, and nationally known character of Thomas Hickathrift. Whilst this story is also seen as a Norfolk tale, I have used the inclusion of the detail that he was born and raised in the Isle of Ely and that he also frequently visited Wisbech, a town where his reputation continued through the centuries, as justification for including the tale within this book. This tale is followed by the poignant account of the Ely and Littleport Riots of 1816, compiled from contemporary and historical accounts; and an exploration of the toadmen, who could control horses, along with a tale of one such a man who came to a particularly gruesome end. The section concludes with tales of people being lost in the landscape, including the tale of a boy who became stuck in the newly drained Whittlesey Mere.

TOM HICKATHRIFT – LEGENDARY GIANT

Here Lubin listened with awestruck surprise.
When Hickathrift's great strength has met his ear;
How he killed giants as they were but flies,

And lifted trees as one would a spear,
Though not much bigger than his fellows were;
He knew no troubles waggoner's have known,
Of getting stalled and such disasters drear;
Up he'd chuck sacks as we would hurl a stone,
And draw whole loads of grain unaided and alone.

John Clare, 'The Village Minstrel XLIV'

In the time before William the Conqueror there dwelt a poor, but hard-working labouring man in the marsh of the Isle of Ely, whose name was Thomas Hickathrift. This man had one son called by his own name and he had worked hard to buy him an education but the younger Tom would have none of it.

When the old man passed from this world, young Tom's mother worked hard to look after her son as best she could. But young Tom was a lazy fellow, who liked nothing better than sitting in the chimney corner, warming his toes and dreaming of his next meal.

For Tom was a big lad, and when he was only 10 years old he was eight feet high, and five feet wide, with hands like shoulders of mutton, and he could eat as much as four or five ordinary men. From top to toe he looked like a giant, but no one knew if he had the strength to match.

One day Tom's mother came home from a hard day's work with her back aching. She had slept badly the night before on her straw mattress, which needed refilling. She told her son that the farmer down the lane had said that they could have a couple of bundles of straw if they could carry them home themselves. She asked her son if he would get this for her, and help her to fill her mattress.

Young Tom swore that he would not go, but his mother begged him, and eventually he agreed, if she could get him something to carry it with.

The old woman came back with some stout cord, but Tom said, 'But Mother, that's no use, I must have a wagon rope.'

She fetched him a cart rope and Tom went on his way to the farmer's house where the man and his workers were busy in the barn. He said to the farmer, 'I am here for a bundle of straw', and the man replied, 'Tom, take as much as you can carry.'

Tom laid down his rope and began to make up the bundle, picking up handful after handful of straw until he had gathered some 20cwt (hundredweight) or as much as a cartload. The farmer watched in amazement as Tom wrapped the rope around the straw and then flung it over his shoulder as if it were a small sack.

The farmer, amazed at what he had seen, decided, while Tom was taking the first load home, to put some stones each weighing a hundredweight into the next load.

Tom didn't notice and one stone dropped out. 'How badly they have cleaned this straw,' he cried. 'There's some of the corn dropping out.' Further on, the other stone dropped out. 'Oh,' he said, 'there's some more corn dropping,' but then he took no further notice.

Word of Tom's strength soon spread and he found that instead of sitting by the fire in the chimney corner, he was being paid to do work lifting and carrying. One day a woodsman asked for his help to clear a tree that was blocking a path. Tom arrived at the place and found four men trying to lift the trunk onto a cart with pulleys. 'Stand away, you fools,' said Tom as he put his foot near the roots, levered the tree onto one end and then laid it in the cart. He then asked for a stick for his mother's fire, and proceeded to pick up a tree bigger than was in the cart, and to carry it home on his shoulders.

As awareness of his great strength spread even further, Tom had many adventures. He fought many fights, lifted and threw many a heavy weight, and won many a contest. And his fame reached the ears of a brewer from King's Lynn, who needed a good strong man to carry his beer to Wisbech. The brewer sought to hire Tom and promised him a new set of clothes each year, a roof over his head (for him and his mother) and as much food and drink as he wanted.

So Tom moved with his mother to King's Lynn and took the job, and each day he would load the cart with beer and carry it to Wisbech, a journey of twenty miles. But something bothered Tom. He had been told by his master that he must not go the quickest way across the marshland as it was occupied by a monstrous giant who killed or made servants of anyone that crossed his path. Whereas this would frighten most people, Tom could not stop thinking of the time that would be saved if he could shorten the journey.

So one day Tom, stronger than ever from a diet of good food and strong ale, decided that he would take the shortcut. As he started to open the gates and lead his cart and horses onto the forbidden path, he reasoned that he was a big man and could take on any giant. But the giant spied him, and came up close.

'Who gave you permission to come this way?' the giant roared. 'How dare you fling my gates open! Don't you care that I kill rogues like you? See how many heads I have hung on yonder tree. Yours will hang higher than the rest.'

But Tom was not going back, 'A turd in your teeth,' he shouted. 'You will not find me like one of them.'

'You are a fool,' said the giant, 'to come here to fight with no weapon to defend yourself.'

'I have a weapon here that will show you to be a rogue and a traitor,' replied Tom as the giant went off to fetch his great club, determined to dash out Tom's brains.

Tom looked around for a weapon, and having nothing to hand took his cart, turned it upside down, and took off the axle-tree to use as a club. He then grabbed a wheel to use as a shield!

A bloody fight ensued that lasted many hours and eventually Tom was victorious. He cut out the giants tongue as proof of the deed, and then went to find out where the giant had hidden all the silver and gold from his victims. He found the hoard, repaired his cart, loaded it with the treasure and continued on his journey to deliver the beer to Wisbech. On the journey he told everyone he met of his adventure.

When Tom returned to King's Lynn, he told his master and the townsfolk, and a great number of them set out to the giant's land to view the dead body and to celebrate. They were overjoyed, for not only had Tom got rid of their great enemy, but he had also cleared the way for them to take the shorter route to Wisbech. The people in the local villages also now had access to some very fertile pasture land.

The news of Tom's victory in killing the giant spread around the country and reached the ears of the king. At this time a man had arrived at court with the giant's head saying he had carried out the deed. The king was confused and called for Tom Hickathrift, who produced the tongue to prove his victory. Tom was rewarded by the king by being made Sir Thomas Hickathrift and was allowed to build himself a fine house on the giant's land between King's Lynn and Wisbech.

Another story says that, some time later, the king needed help in destroying a giant and many great lions and bears who had invaded the Isle of Thanet in Kent. The king made Tom the governor of

Thanet, and sent him off to fight the invaders. This giant was more intimidating than his marshland cousin, and mounted upon a dreadful dragon. He had just one eye in the middle of his forehead, and appeared like a flaming fire.

But Tom was not daunted and soon ran his ten-feet-long two-handed sword in between the giant's brawny buttocks, and out through his belly. He then pulled out his sword and, with six or seven blows, he cut off the giant's head. Tom then killed the dragon and the rest of the beasts before returning to Wisbech, where he married and lived happily to the end of his days.

A rhyme referring to Tom Hickathrift was found throughout the district until quite recently:

> *He ate a cow and a calf,*
> *an ox and a half,*
> *the church and the steeple,*
> *and then all the people,*
> *and yet had not enough.*

The story is an adaptation of a tale printed in a seventeenth-century chapbook, *The History of Thomas Hickathrift*, in the Pepysian Library from around 1600. This and a later version found in the British Library were compared by the folklorist G.L. Gomme in 1885.

It has been speculated that the stories of Hickathrift, with the axle and the wheel and other motifs, may have Norse roots; the drinking bout could be linked to the exploits of Thor. Others have noted the links with the tale of Jack the Giant Killer. The historical roots of this story, and one of its main pieces of evidence, is from John Weever's *Ancient Funerall Monuments* (1631), which states that at one time a great conflict broke out between the local people and the landlord over a piece of fine pastureland of about 1,200 acres known as 'The Smeeth'. This common land had been shared by the people of the Seven Towns of Marshland, namely Walpole

St Peter, Walsoken, West Walton, Terrington, Clenchwarton, Emneth and Tilney. During this conflict Tom Hickathrift had a job carting beer for a King's Lynn brewer and had to drive his cart across this land:

> perceiving that his neighbours were faint-hearted, and ready to take flight ... [he] shook the axle-tree from the cart, which he used instead of a sword, and took one of the cart-wheels which he held as a buckler ... he set upon the ... adversaries of the Common, encouraged his neighbours to go forward, and fight valiantly in defence of their liberties; who being animated by his manly prowess, they ... chased the landlord and his company, to the utmost verge of the said Common; which from that time they have quietly enjoyed to this very day.

The memory of the legend is still preserved in local place and property names. Hickathrift House is a care home situated in Marshland St James, a parish established on the former common land of The Smeeth in the 1930s.

Hickathrift Farm is nearby and a field opposite is called Hickathrift's Field, in which there was once a mound and two hollows, or ponds, that were known as the giant's bath and wash basin (or punchbowl or feeding bowl). Sadly, the hollows were filled in with earth from the mound in March 1929 to prepare the land for building council houses.

A story used to be told of how Tom Hickathrift once stood on the bank of a river three miles away and threw a stone declaring that where it landed he wished to be buried. The eight-feet-long stone, on which there used to be carved a cross within a circle (to represent the axle and the wheel), is said to have bounced off the roof of the church to its present site.

According to the Marshland St James website, some old slate writings were found in an excavation and were buried under what is now the village sign, at Hickathrift's Corner, on the junction of Smeeth Road and School Road, in 1976. The writings, it is said, contained the curse of the Hickathrift giant and these slates had been 'broken into fragments and cast over Marshland Fen in order that Tom could continue after death as he had done in life … protecting the area from intruders'. The wording was believed to have been similar to:

Whomsoever cometh to smote or siege this fen with arms or ill intended shall leave it or leave it in pain or on pain of death for I Tom Hickathrift shall remain a guardian and beareth my right to defend.

The village sign for Marshland St James depicts Tom, as does that of Tilney All Saints. The former has a base that incorporates one of Hickathrift's candlesticks. Two more of these 'candlesticks' (actually the uprights of old memorial crosses) can be found in the churchyard at Tilney All Saints. Also in the churchyard, close to the south wall, is an oval stone that is known as the giant's gravestone. This stone is visited by many and is clearly signed as to its contents. However, the original gravestone appears to have been removed to inside the church and the stone outside is relatively new.

In Wisbech and district there can still be found a number of variants and additions to the stories of Thomas Hickathrift. He seems to have been responsible for kicking balls and damaging many of the local churches. A good source for some of these are on the Hidden East Anglia website.

This website includes speculation by Mike Burgess, a historian, that there may have been a real person on whom the character of Tom Hickathrift was based. Sir Frederick de Tilney, a giant of a man with great strength, was a medieval knight who performed 'prodigies of valour' for his king. Sir Frederick's main home was at Boston in Lincolnshire, and he may have championed the villagers of the Marshland in a dispute with their local landlord over rights to the use of common land.

Mike also theorised that after Sir Frederick's death the story of the 'wicked landlord' was altered over time to the battle between an evil ogre against Hickathrift, a misremembering of Sir Frederick. In the way of oral storytelling, the story gathered ingredients from the stock of legend of the people, including that of the Norse tradition, which had a strong influence in the area.

Old maps indicate that the 1,200 acres of common land known as The Smeeth were once shared by the people of the Seven Towns of Marshland, namely Walpole St Peter, Walsoken, West Walton, Terrington, Clenchwarton, Emneth and Tilney.

THE ELY AND LITTLEPORT RIOTS

For many years, children in the Ely and Littleport area sang the following song:

> *A starving crowd, singing loud*
> *For higher pay, rued the day*
> *When a Bishop's cope, a hangman's rope*
> *And a Butcher's cart, all played their part*
> *As those Littleport men saw the last of the fen*
> *From that knacker's yard in Ely*
> *Until book and bell are sold in Hell*
> *Fenmen will never forget or forgive …*

This song recalls events that took place in the year 1816. This story remembers these events, known as the Ely and Littleport Riots, and uses as its sources two tales from W.H. Barrett along with the historical record. The first of Barrett's tales was from William 'Chafer' Legge who was told the tale by his grandfather, who he said actually witnessed the events of history unfold. The second source is from the transcript of 'Old Pygall's Story', recorded from Barrett at Framingham Pigot, Norfolk, and broadcast on BBC Radio in July 1960.

A bad year, 1816. It was described as 'the year without summer', a year when it constantly rained, and the temperature failed to rise sufficiently for the crops to ripen. Scientists would later say that this was due to a volcanic eruption in Indonesia, but that knowledge wouldn't have helped the people when the harvest failed and the price of bread continued to rise to beyond their means. The poor were forced to eat nettles and what could be found in the hedgerows. Many were starving.

Large numbers of men had returned from fighting in the Napoleonic Wars and they expected a better life. They had won the Battle of Waterloo and were proud to be English, proud to come home. But not when they saw the price of bread and the hungry people.

The government was also worried. They remembered the French Revolution and feared that something similar might happen in England. They were aware that the returning soldiers knew the tactics of battle and how to defend themselves, and also to feed themselves from the produce of the land, the air and the water. They had also learned that if their wages were not paid, they could get their rewards through looting.

Of the people who weren't trained soldiers, many had to look for other ways to feed and care for themselves and, on 22 May 1816, fifty or sixty people of the Benefits Club met at The Globe Inn in Littleport to decide who should receive payments from the fund to which they all subscribed: they found that most of the people were in need of some form of help.

So the members decided to ask the wealthy farmers for bigger donations or for a rise in wages. But of course the wealthy farmers were not able to help. They said that the price of bread affected them too.

The discussion in The Globe that night became heated and one man went out to blow a horn to summon the rest of the people. Eventually a big crowd gathered and they heard how in the riots in Norfolk, and at Downham Market, the people had been given higher wages. They wanted this too, and they wanted it immediately.

So the people went to the house of John Vachell, the vicar, who was also a magistrate, and asked him for help, but he threatened to shoot the first man who crossed his threshold. The people took no notice of this and barged their way in. He offered them £1 and some beer but they said this wasn't enough and started to search his house for whatever they could find. They did not notice when the vicar, and his wife and children, sneaked out of the back of the vicarage onto the road, where they managed to get a ride in a carriage to Ely, and to report the troubles that were going on.

The rioters also went to the house of Henry Martin, the main landowner in the district, to demand higher wages and money for the poor. He managed to slip out before they got there, leaving his old mother and his brother to watch as the house was ransacked.

Later, some men stopped a stage coach that was going through the town and demanded money from the occupants. They did not notice that it was Henry Martin inside the coach, as they were more interested in the small amount of money he gave them. But Henry later used the incident as evidence of highway robbery.

By about four o'clock in the morning between 150 and 200 people, both men and women, had gathered together and decided to march five miles south to Ely. They hoped that there, in the cathedral city, they might get agreement for higher wages, or the lowering of the price of bread.

They got a farm cart and horses to pull it, and they turned it into a gun platform by fixing a couple of fowling guns 'fore' and 'aft'. But as they reached the outskirts of Ely they were met by the Revd Metcalfe and Revd Ward, both of whom were justices of the peace, and who offered to give in to their demands if they would just return to their homes.

The people had come so far that they did not want to go straight home; they wanted to spend time in the market, and to ensure that their demands would be met. The magistrates told them to gather in the marketplace where a public announcement would be made.

So the rioters of Littleport came into the city to be joined by local people, and they listened as the Revd Metcalfe called out

from the window of The White Hart that the magistrates agreed
to the demands for higher wages so that the people could afford to
buy bread. Metcalfe then asked that they all return to their homes.

Many people did go home, but some of the Littleport people
stayed in Ely where, it was said, some of the landlords were offering
free drinks. By this time some of the younger rioters had also had
rather a lot to drink, and the looting that had started in Littleport
continued in Ely.

Little did the people know, that not only were the local militia
being sworn in, but troops had also been called from Bury
St Edmunds and Royston. A letter to London said that a 'politically motivated' riot was taking place.

By noon of the following day the troops had arrived, headed by
Sir Henry Bate Dudley, who was not just a magistrate and a canon
of Ely Cathedral, but also a good friend of the Prince Regent. The
Riot Act had been read at various times to try to stop the rioting
but to no avail. Dudley now led the Dragoons into Ely and quelled
the rioting there. He also made many arrests before he travelled on
to Littleport.

By this time, most of the Littleport people had made it back
home and were gathered in The George and Dragon public house,
where they had also built a crude barricade of tables and chairs.
Dudley ordered that some of his troops go round to the east of the
town, whilst the others approached from the south-west. By the
time they reached Main Street they were going at a hard gallop.
When they got to The George and Dragon, Dudley read the Riot
Act again and ordered the men to surrender.

The men took no notice, and Dudley tried to barge his way
in, but he was stopped by two men. Shots were fired from inside
the pub and one of the militia was hit. This man who had fought
bravely at Waterloo and come out unscathed was now injured by
one of his own countrymen. Invalided, his arm shot to bits, he
would live off the parish for the rest of his days.

The men who were inside The George and Dragon finally came
out, where they were soon surrounded. One of them tried to grab a

gun and to make a run for it, but as he escaped he was shot through the back of the head. It is said that the bullet came out through his eye socket and embedded itself one and a half inches into the brick wall.

The daily coach arrived and there were screams as the people saw the dead man lying in a pool of blood, and another man with the bottom of his chin cut off being roughly bandaged, as he was carried away to Ely gaol.

All except one of the people arrested were men. When they got to Ely there were eighty-six people crowded into the small gaol awaiting their fate. Dudley and the other magistrates rode to London to confirm that the riots were politically motivated, and it was agreed that the trial would be a Special Commission Assizes to set an example to others who tried to riot. The date of the special assizes was set for four weeks after the riots. In all this time those accused were kept in the gaol.

In the run-up to the trial Chafer Legge's grandfather worked from dawn to dusk so that he could take time off to watch the proceedings. He was there on the first morning of the trial, as the elaborate carriages arrived from London and men in fine clothing got out to be welcomed by the Bishop of Ely. These men were invited into the Bishop's Palace, where it is said that they enjoyed a hearty breakfast.

Crowds of local people also watched as the men came out of the palace and went into the cathedral. They could hear a service going on and were told that it was to help the judges to make the right decision. In time, the judges and attendants came out of the cathedral and walked to the Sessions House. There was not enough room inside for the crowds to watch, so they stood outside to watch for the arrival of their friends from the gaol.

The accused were finally brought to the Sessions House and taken inside to await their fate, in a trial that lasted six days. Each day, Chafer Legge's grandfather walked from Littleport to Ely to support those condemned and to listen and look for signs of any progress. At the end of the trial, the people heard that twenty-four men and one woman had been convicted of capital offences. They were stunned when they heard the news.

Chafer Legge's grandfather and others discussed ways to help their friends, as some had done in the time between the riots and the arrests, but now they realised that all was lost. They then heard that no one in Ely would agree to make the coffins and that the authorities had to get someone from Cambridge to make them. It was also said that the man who provided refreshments for the carpenters constructing the new scaffold had both his legs broken whilst out 'on the fen'.

The day of the execution arrived, 28 June. Crowds flocked to Ely to watch as the condemned were brought out of the gaol and put on a two-wheeled cart, a tumbril, where they had to sit on their own coffins. Chafer's grandfather had expected lots of carts but then he heard that of the twenty-four convicted, mercy had been granted to all but five men. The others had received a commutation of the death sentence and were now to remain in prison or be transported.

Everyone watched as the horses, draped with black and with black plumes, pulled the cart. They saw hundreds of the 'great and good' arrive, many of whom had been at the trial. They saw the procession form, and the richly dressed men carrying white wands, proceed for nearly two hours from the gaol to the place of execution.

A sermon was then preached to the enormous crowd in front of the gallows. In fact it was repeated so that those who took longer to find their places could also hear it. Meanwhile, the condemned men listened to the description of their acts as being politically motivated. Yet the local people knew that it was about the price of food and inadequate wages, and that drink had fuelled the looting. Nothing more than that!

Eventually the order was given, the trap was dropped, and the men fell to their deaths. People crowded forward to pull on their legs to hasten their passing. After a short time, the bodies were cut down and carried to a nearby house where they were laid in their coffins and people were allowed to pay their last respects to those who had died bravely, like true Fenmen.

Some of the old men from Littleport and Southery cut off little bits of the ropes that still hung around the necks and gave them to the gathered people as a mark of remembrance of those who had died over the price of food. They also made the people swear over the coffins that they would 'tell their children, generation after generation, about what the Bishop and the gentry had done to those Fenmen who'd only done when they were drunk what the college lads had done many a time in Cambridge without anything being done about it'.

And when the people from Littleport finally returned to their homes they found that five swans had taken up residence around the village. The swans stayed for a long time and all who saw them liked to take comfort in the belief that they were the souls of those dead men.

Those men who were to be transported were given no time to say farewell to their loved ones before they were taken to Newgate in London on Monday 1 July, and then moved to a prison ship to await the long voyage to Botany Bay, Australia.

Those who had been sentenced to one year in Ely gaol also found themselves urgently carried to Sheerness where they served their time on a prison ship. Protests by local people, who had also not been allowed time to say goodbye, did not alter this decision. When the prisoners were released in June 1817, however, the government 'very liberally allowed' each of them sufficient money to get home.

In time, more as a warning than a mark of respect, a plaque was placed on the wall of St Mary's Church, Ely, inscribed as follows:

Here lye interned in one grave the Bodies of: William Beamiss, George Crow, John Dennis, Isaac Harley, and Thomas South, who were all executed at Ely on the 28th Day of June 1816 having been convicted at the special Assizes holden there of diverse Robberies during the Riots at Ely and Littleport in the Month of May in that year. May their awful Fate be a warning to others.

Research, and comments made by W.H. Barrett seem to indicate that the site of the gallows is now the recreation ground opposite St John's School, Ely. To commemorate the Queen's Silver Jubilee in 1977 the Women's Institute in Littleport paid for a village sign that includes a depiction of the start of the riot outside The Globe Inn. Plaques have also been placed around the town at other significant sites.

I do not know if there are still toadmen in the Fens, but there certainly were at one time, and that was not so long ago. These were ordinary men who had carried out an elaborate ritual so that they could gain power over horses and other strange supernatural powers.

It is said that this ritual involved catching a male toad and either skinning it alive or pegging it to an ant hill so that the ants could pick the bones clean. The bones would then be carried on the person until they were fully dried. At midnight when the moon was shining, the initiate would go to a stream and throw the bones into the water. The bones would then let out a terrifying scream as they floated downstream, whilst just one of the bones would float in the opposite direction, also screaming. This bone would be removed from the water and carried by the toadman who believed that he had, by his actions, made a pact with the Devil. One account even adds that the toadman must carry the bone into the stables at midnight for three consecutive nights, and on the final night he would actually meet with and fight the Devil.

It is not surprising that people would be wary of such toadmen, particularly as they could stop horses from moving an inch or make them unmanageable for anyone else. The tutor organiser for the WEA adult education initiative in Fenland in the 1950s, G.W. Pattison, researched the subject for a paper that he sent to the Folklore Society. He was told a story about a toadman who sat down at night in a loft while a chaff cutter worked itself, and also of a toadman who became so frightened as a result of his experiences that he left the land and went to work in a factory.

He was also informed of what happened when a person who worked alongside toadmen tried to find out their secret – the answer was likely to be: 'I daren't tell my own son. What I know goes to the churchyard with me.' Another informant explained that their own father had expressed a desire to become a toadman, but was dissuaded by his father (the informant's grandfather) that if he did 'he would shoot him'.

An example of the toadman's power can be gauged from a tale told in Ely of how a carter on a farm was told to take a wagon into Cambridge. He set out early before anyone else was up and about, but when the farmer went into the yard he found that the horses were still in the stable, yet the wagon had gone. On searching around he found that some young horses, not yet broken for cart work, were also missing. The farmer and his workers fully expected the carter to return from an unsuccessful trip; however, very late that night the horses arrived back at the stables with the wagon containing the carter who was dead drunk and sound asleep. No one ever solved the mystery of how the carter managed to harness and drive such inexperienced horses and get them back safely.

The following story, about a toadman in the Chatteris area, is based on three variants of the same story, two of which were collected in north Lincolnshire in the 1880s (and were combined in the tale of 'Fred the Fool' in my *Lincolnshire Folk Tales* book), and the third collected by Polly Howat in the 1990s in a Wisbech nursing home from a very elderly woman who had been told the story by her grandfather.

A key part of the story is the 'Chief Worm', which may be derived from the Anglo Saxon 'wyrm', which means dragon. In the Norse tradition, Nidhogg the dragon lives in Hel, the realm of the dead under the Guardian Tree, Yggdrasill, where he eats the bodies of the dead.

ELIJAH'S GHOST (A TALE OF A TOADMAN)

Long ago, a farmer went to the Michaelmas hiring fair to find someone to help him to manage his horses. He found a young man named Elijah, who seemed competent and invited him to work at his farm, which was situated on Acre Fen between Chatteris and Somersham.

Elijah became a 'live in' labourer and soon proved very skilled at handling the horses that pulled the plough. The farmer, however, though he fed his workers adequately, was not good at parting with his money and was often late with the wages.

So, in response to the late payment, Elijah decided to teach the farmer a lesson and he used his toadman's ability to stop the horses from working. The farmer was furious with this but he could not get the horses to move an inch until he had paid everyone what was due.

From that day on, the relationship between Elijah and the farmer changed and the latter became suspicious if anything went wrong. His fear continued to increase and, as a result of this, the young man became more aloof, until one night the farmer crept into the small hut where the toadman was sleeping soundly and, using a pair of pliers, pulled off one of his nails.

Elijah surprisingly did nothing, and got up the next morning and carried on with his work. However, a while later a joint of meat went missing and, though the other farm labourers said that they had seen the dog eating the meat, the farmer blamed the toadman and in his anger swung an axe that chopped off the young man's arm.

Realising what he had done, the farmer offered Elijah a small amount of compensation and a couple of days off, which seemed to settle the situation. However, the farmer was still wary of the toadman's power, and when a week or two later he was woken by shouts from the stack yard and found his barn – full of hay – blazing furiously, his only thoughts were that Elijah had started the fire in revenge.

The farmer rushed to the hut, grabbed Elijah by the throat and dragged him to the fire, where without a word he flung him into the flames.

When the embers had died down, the spirit of the young man found himself walking in the netherworld and he asked the creatures there what he should do next. He was told that he would need to see the Chief Worm who would eat him up so that his spirit could rest in peace.

Elijah found his way to the Chief Worm but was told that he would need to return with his ashes. He did so but was told that there was still something missing. Recalling that he had lost his arm he was told that he must retrieve that too.

Fortunately the arm had been carefully buried near the farm and the toadman was able to bring the partially decomposed arm to the worm, but this was still not sufficient. The worm could smell that the nail was missing.

Sadly Elijah could not locate the missing nail and so he was destined to wander in the twilight space for the rest of eternity, and it is here that the great-grandfather of the old lady saw him … a ghostly figure, walking out on the Acre Fen in a haze of green light …

The Legend of Whittlesey Mere

The following story is adapted from an account in *Fenland Notes & Queries* in 1891. It had originally been published in 1887 in *Leisure Hour*, and had been taken directly from the 'principal actor'. In this adaptation I have tried to keep the 'Victorian' feel!

In 1851, on a Sunday afternoon in February, a cottager's son from Holme was employed in bird scaring on Holme Fen, part of what was once Whittlesey Mere.

The mere had been drained by this time but was still surrounded by what was known as 'the reed shore', a belt of reed surrounding the mere like a miniature forest, the reeds growing to a height of fourteen feet and upwards. This reed shore was a great source of revenue to its proprietors, reeds being used for thatching.

WHITTLESEA MERE, FROM YAXLEY - 1851

The little boy, so intent on his task, wandered from his normal position through the reed shore and onto the dried bed of the mere. He had taken no more than a few steps when he began to sink, with no power to extricate himself and no one near to render him assistance, or even see his predicament.

Luckily he had not ventured more than a yard from what was, comparatively speaking, dry land, and although he kept on sinking inch by inch, and expected that the mud would soon be over his head, he stopped sinking when the mud had reached his armpits.

It was then half-past three in the afternoon, and the boy, firmly stuck in the mud, could hear the Connington Church clock to mark the time and count the hours. He could also hear the trains on the Great Northern Railway, the times of which he was familiar with. The boy also shouted for help, but there was no one near to aid him, nor would there be until the next morning.

The evening soon closed in, followed by a night that was not only very dark, but very tempestuous. The boy, who ceased calling for help, was not overpowered by fatigue or cold, but remained awake and sensible the whole of the night.

The next morning the young lad could see one or two labourers in the distance, but found himself not just powerless from the cold, but unable to make any sign to them. At ten o'clock he heard a man on the other side of the reed bed, but he had no voice to call him. When the sound of the man died away, the boy began to think that his last hope was gone.

Half an hour later, the boy again heard the man pushing amongst the reeds, and in a marvellously providential way the man's footsteps were guided to the very spot were the boy's head, shoulders and arms were seen above the bed of the mud. The astonishment of the man at the sight may be more easily imagined than described.

With great difficulty, the man released the boy from his painful position, and carried him through the reed shore on to the firm land. By this time, the lad was completely paralysed with cold, and unable to speak, having spent nineteen hours in the mud.

Fortunately, as the man too came from Holme, he recognised the boy and took him home, much to the surprise of his parents, who had accounted for his absence by assuming that he had gone to the neighbouring village of Sawtry to see his grandmother, and that she had kept him for the night.

A surgeon from Stilton was quickly fetched, and the boy was promptly attended to. For two days he seemed to feel acutely the effect of his time in the mud, but the following week he was back in school, apparently none the worse for his misfortune.

A not dissimilar story occurred a century earlier when Matthew Wyldbore, a former MP for Peterborough, was out walking on the common that borders the Fens. Suddenly a dense fog came down and Matthew could not find his way. He was afraid to move in case he stumbled into a cross-drain or fen dyke, when he began to hear the ringing of the bells of St John's Church in Peterborough. The bells helped him to locate his position and he returned in safety to the city and his home in the Mansion House in Westgate (now part of The Bull Hotel).

Mr Wyldbore was particularly fond of bell ringing (and was also a good amateur singer) and when he died on 15 March 1781 he left particular instructions in his will to enable the ringers of the Peterborough Parish Church of St John the Baptist to ring one peal or more of the same bells on that day annually. He also left money for an annual sermon and for an allowance of bread for the poor. Mr Wyldbore was buried in his favourite church, where there is a memorial to his memory within the Lady Chapel.

The tradition of Matthew Wyldbore's Day is still recognised by the Parish Church of St John the Baptist on 15 March each year when the bells ring a quarter peal at 6 p.m. A sermon is also still preached, and in 2014 money was raised to support the local food bank.

A similar tale to that of Wyldbore has become attached to St Ives and Hemingford Grey. Both parishes have a trust that was set up by St Ives resident Robert Langley in 1656. In his will, Langley left land in the Isle of Ely, from which the rent would be used to help the poor and particularly the bell ringers. A tale evolved that Langley was lost in the snow on Hemingford Meadow whilst walking from St Ives to Godmanchester, when he heard the church bells ringing. The sound helped him find his way to safety.

Sadly, there is no mention of such an occurrence in his will, which merely states that he made the bequest to commemorate the death of his father. Like the Wyldbore tradition, the Langley trust still distributes food to parishioners.

Today, Holme Fen is the largest remaining lowland birch woodland in the UK. On the edge of the former Whittlesey Mere, which was retained after the initial Fenland drainage in the seventeenth century, the land was unsuitable for ploughing.

After Whittlesey Mere was successfully drained by 1851, the reedbed, raised bog and fen habitat dried out and collapsed over time and this led to the formation of the birch-dominated woodland.

Shortly after draining the mere, W. Wells, the man largely responsible for the drainage, sunk a post – known as the Holme Fen Post – into the peat so that the top was at ground level. By 1870 the top of the post was eight feet above the ground, and by 1938 it had reached eleven feet.

A new post with a concrete base was erected in 1960 and marked to show the previous shrinkage. Today this post now sits at about twelve feet (four metres) above ground level, a marker to show the phenomenal rate of shrinkage over the decades.

In 2001, an ambitious project was commenced with the aim of creating a rich fenland landscape between and around the two National Nature Reserves of Holme Fen (the lowest place in England, lying over seven feet (two metres) below sea level) and nearby Woodwalton Fen. The Great Fen Project was initiated by Natural England, working in partnership with the Environment Agency, the Wildlife Trust, Huntingdonshire District Council and the Middle Level Commission.

To date the project has managed to acquire almost 1,500ha (approximately 60 per cent of the total project area) of land, which is now under conservation management. It is planned that the wider project will incorporate flood storage areas to provide further protection for surrounding farmland from flood events.

The project aims to significantly increase the wildlife interest of the local area and provide opportunities for tourism, which will benefit the regional economy. Local communities are also being encouraged to help develop the Great Fen Project through volunteering, land management and helping people to appreciate the wildlife that surrounds them. A website giving further details of the project can be found at www.greatfen.org.uk.

2

OF STRANGE
PHENOMENA

The subject of this chapter is the weird occurrences that have been recorded in Cambridgeshire. Commencing with the story of how Mr Leech of Raveley made a bargain with the Devil, an allegedly true seventeenth-century account included by W.H. Bernard Saunders in his *Legends and Traditions of Huntingdonshire* (1888). Mr Saunders included the exact text from a pamphlet published in 1662, and it is this that I have translated and edited, but without changing the truthfulness of the tale.

The chapter continues with some of the varied tales connected with Robin Good-fellow, the offspring of Oberon, King of the Fairies and a mortal woman. His name is immortalised in an ancient lane that runs from the centre of the Fenland town of March on to the fen. A collection of short tales about supernatural night-time experiences will then be explored before the final tale, which concerns an event that is alleged to have happened near Red Mere in medieval times.

Mr Leech and the Devil

Mr John Leech of Raveley in Huntingdonshire was going to a fair with a resolution to drink there with some of his friends, but before he had got even two miles from his own house, he met a neighbour and persuaded him to go along and drink his morning draught with him.

The neighbour was reluctant and pleaded that he had a great deal of business to do that day, but Mr Leech was not satisfied with that answer, and forced him into the alehouse.

The two men started drinking together, and it was not long before Mr Leech, being almost drunk, began to behave very merrily, until his friend asked the people of the house what time it was.

When they were told that it was almost eleven o'clock, Mr Leech replied, 'Then let the Devil take him who goes out of this house today.'

A short while after this, Mr Leech changed his mind, and said he must go to the fair, which was to be held at Whittlesey, but his friend said to him, 'Do you not remember the oath you made just now?'

'Ha, ha, ha,' said Mr Leech. 'I'll warrant you the Devil will not trouble me, besides I am so heavy, he'll not be able to carry me halfway to the fair.'

'But he'll be able to carry you to your journey's end somewhere else,' replied his neighbour.

'I'll risk it,' said Mr Leech, who called for his horse and took his leave of his friend.

Mr Leech then rode on towards the fair, but he hadn't got more than two miles from the alehouse when he began to remember the oath that he had sworn and broken, and became extremely troubled in his conscience, and began to consider turning round and riding home. He continued thinking like this and arguing with himself, and riding back and forth, for some time, with his conscience sorely troubled at the damnable oath he had taken, and then broken.

As night began to fall, he continued to ride backwards and forwards, but by then he had no idea of his whereabouts until, at about one or two o'clock in the morning, he saw two grim and terrifying creatures before him, in the likeness of griffins.

He then heard a terrible voice, which said three times, 'Remember your sins and the oath you have broken this day.'

As he heard this, Mr Leech fell from his horse to the ground, as if he were in a trance, and then he felt himself very roughly handled between the two griffins, who carried him swiftly through the air for more than twelve miles from that place, over a great water called Whittlesey Mere, and Ramsey Mere to a town called Doddington, and there dropped him in Patron's Yard, without either clothes or sense.

The next morning, the servants who making their ploughs and harrows fit for work, found Mr Leech, a sad spectacle, apparently all bloody and gored by the harrows. Being very much astonished at the sight, the people demanded to know how Mr Leech came there, who he was, and where he lived.

Mr Leech was unable to answer them with anything but sighs and groans, and the servants, very much disturbed by the poor man's condition, ran in and informed their master who came out to look for himself.

On seeing the condition of Mr Leech, the master ordered that a bed be made up and the poor man laid in it, and for him to be covered and kept very warm.

When this was done, Mr Leech began to recover his senses and told them the whole story of who he was, where he lived, where he had been going, and how he came to be there. He also expressed his desire that he might be allowed to rest for another day or two there, and his wish was granted by the good gentleman.

In the meantime, some of the servants of the house who were going about their business in the vicinity, just two miles away found by chance some torn clothes, which they brought home, supposing them to be his.

But when they showed the clothes to him, he recognised them and grew into a frenzy, so desperate that they were afraid to stay in his chamber.

The gentleman of the house asked Mr Leech if he would like them to send for the minister to pray by him, but he was given a very desperate answer.

When Mr Leech said 'I am past his recovery', the gentleman, very much troubled at this answer, sent privately to the parson of the town with a request for him to come to him presently.

The minister arrived in all haste at the gentleman's house, and was told about the sad case. On hearing the details, the minister desired that he might be allowed to go up to see Mr Leech alone, so that he could see what he could do towards the recovery of the man's soul, which he feared at that time was in very great danger.

No sooner had the minister entered into his chamber than Mr Leech rose out of his bed, ran towards him and violently threw him on the ground (which could have cost the minister his life) saying, 'What business have you here?'

The minister tried (as well as he could) to comfort the faithless man, but the noise of what had occurred had been heard downstairs, and the people were afraid that Mr Leech might harm the minister. Their fears proved true when they went up to assist, for they found Mr Leech beating the parson with all the strength he had.

The servants got hold of Mr Leech by both his arms, bound them and laid him in his bed; and when he found himself bound he made a terrible noise and broke his bindings, whereupon the people grew afraid of him and rushed out and locked the door.

No one dared to go into his chamber that day or night, and the next morning when they went to the door to listen to see if they could hear him stir, they could not hear any noise.

Supposing Mr Leech to be asleep they opened the door, but they found him on the bed with his neck broke, his tongue out of his mouth, and his body as black as coal, all swollen, and every bone in his body out of joint.

The sad spectacle was viewed by many of the local people, before the stench of it became too great and the body was eventually buried. The most important men of the town who saw the sad sight wrote a witness statement to confirm what they had seen. Those who signed it were John Webber, Gentleman; Jeffery Hobkins, Gentleman; Robert Shipton, Gentleman; Francis Hall, Yeoman; James Smith, Yeoman; Thomas Cracroft, Yeoman.

Mr Saunders noted the age of the account and criticised the content. He remarked that Mr Leech was said to have been carried across 'Whittlesey Mere and Ramsey Mere' and that this would have been a very round-about way to travel from Raveley or Whittlesey to Doddington. This would have made the distance considerably more than 'twelve miles'. He theorised that the course of twelve miles from Doddington over the two meres would have meant a start from somewhere like Yaxley.

He also remarked that Mr Leech being found amongst the harrows could have explained his injuries and the admission that he was 'almost drunk' when he went for his morning's draught, and that by eleven o'clock 'he began to be very merry' could indicate that Mr Leech had been suffering from *delirium tremens*.

Doddington historian David Edwards carried out some research on this story about ten years ago but his search for the gentlemen and yeomen was unsuccessful. The men were not listed in either the parish registers or the hearth tax returns and there is no record of the burial of John Leech. David has come to the conclusion that the man may have died in Duddington near Stamford.

ROBIN GOOD-FELLOW

When house or hearth doth sluttish lye,
I pinch the maidens black and blue;
The bed-clothes from the bed pull I,
And lay them naked all to view.
'Twixt sleep and wake,
I do them take,
And on the key-cold floor them throw.
If out they cry, Then forth I fly,
And loudly laugh out, ho, ho, ho!

Thomas Percy, 1765

In the Fenland market town of March can be found Robingoodfellow's Lane, an ancient trackway that once led over Norwood Common, but which was stopped and rerouted to Norwood Road when the railway was constructed in the 1840s. No one today knows the origins of the name but it could be connected to the household fairy that is also known as a puck or a hobgoblin, and indeed, to the north of the town there is a bridge known as Hobbs Lot Bridge. As this book of folk tales is lacking any other fairy content, I have taken the liberty of recounting some of the popular tales found in *The Mad Pranks and Merry Jests of Robin Goodfellow* (1628).

I will start with the tale of the birth of Robin Good-fellow and explore his childhood before moving on to one of the tales that shows his supposed power of being able to turn himself into a likeness of any person or creature he chose …

ROBINGOODFELLOW'S LANE

The birth and childhood of Robin Good-fellow

Once upon a time, a great while ago, when men ate more and drank less, there were many, sometimes invisible, harmless spirits called fairies, dancing in fairy rings on green hills with sweet music.

Many mad pranks would they play, such as pinching people black and blue and misplacing things in ill-ordered houses; but they would also be kind to those who kept their houses clean, giving them silver and other pretty trinkets, which they would leave for them, sometimes in their shoes, other times in their pockets, sometimes in clean dishes.

Amongst these creatures there was a high fairy: whether he was their king or not I don't know, but he had great control in their realm, as you shall hear.

This high fairy did love a proper young wench (a human), and every night he would, with other fairies, come to the house and dance in her chamber; and often she would dance with him, and at his departure he would leave her silver and jewels to express his love of her.

In time, this maid found herself to be with child, and when she was asked who the father was she answered, 'It is a man that nightly came to visit me, but early in the morning he would go his way. I don't know where he went, he went so suddenly.'

Many old women said that a fairy had got her with child, and that she should take comfort, for the child will be fortunate to have so noble a father, and should be able to work many strange wonders.

In time she was delivered of a boy, who (it should seem) so pleased his father that every night his mother was supplied with the necessary things that are befitting a young mother, and fine things they were too: rich embroidered cushions, stools, carpets, coverlets and delicate linen.

The father of the baby would also leave fine meats: capons, chickens, mutton, lamb, pheasant, woodcock, partridge and quail. The gossips also enjoyed this food, and the maid never wanted company, or people who could help her enjoy the fine wines and sweetmeats that were also delivered.

Everyone praised the honest fairy for his caring ways, and the child for his beauty, and the mother for being a happy woman.

And so the baby was christened and there was such good cheer at the ceremony that many ended up sleeping in their day clothes and could not even remember what name had been given to the child. Luckily the clerk had written it in his book.

Such was the birth and early days of little Robin Good-fellow.

When Robin was 6 years of age, he was so mischievous that all the neighbours complained about him; for no sooner was his mother's back turned than he was up to something or other, so that his mother was forced to take him with her to market, or wherever else she went.

His mother grew tired of the many complaints about Robin, but she didn't know how to beat him justly for it, because she never saw him do things that deserved such punishment. But when the complaints continued day after day, eventually his mother promised him a whipping.

Robin, not surprisingly, did not like that idea, and therefore, to avoid it, he ran away and left his mother alone and sad.

How Robin Good-fellow dwelt with a tailor

After Robin Good-fellow had gone a great distance from his mother's house he began to get hungry, so he knocked on the door of a tailor's house, and begged for food.

The tailor gave him meat and, realising that the boy had no occupation, he took him on as an apprentice. Robin learned his work so well that he gained his master's respect, but eventually Robin showed that he could not stop his old mischievous ways.

On evening the master had a gown to finish for a woman, and it had to be done that night. Both he and Robin sat up late and by twelve o' clock they had done all but setting on the sleeves.

The master then, being sleepy said, 'Robin will you just whip on the sleeves, and then you can go to bed: I am too tired to work any longer.'

'I will', said Robin, but as soon as his master was gone, he hung up the gown, and taking both sleeves in his hands, he whipped and lashed them on the gown.

He was still standing there in the morning when his master came down and asked him what he was doing?

'Why,' said Robin, 'I am doing as you asked me, whipping on the sleeves!'

'You rogue,' said his master, 'I meant that you should sew the sleeves on quickly!'

'I wish you had said that,' said Robin, 'for then I would not have lost the night's sleep.'

Well, to cut a long story short, his master was forced to repair the dress, but before he had finished the task, the woman came to fetch it.

The tailor, trying to keep her happy, asked Robin to fetch some of the remnants from the day before (meaning the meat that was left); but Robin, to annoy his master even more, brought down the remnants of the cloth that was left of the gown.

At the sight of this, his master looked pale, but the woman just sent Robin for wine. Robin never returned again to the tailor's house.

What happened to Robin Good-fellow after he went from the tailor

After Robin had travelled a good day's journey from his master's house he sat down and, being weary, he fell asleep.

No sooner had slumber taken full possession of him, and closed his long-opened eyelids, but he thought he saw many good people in old-fashioned clothes dancing around him, and he heard beautiful music. But such delights never last long, and he woke up to find, lying beside him, a scroll on which were written the following lines, in golden letters:

Robin, my only son and heir,
How to live take thou no care:
By nature thou has cunning shifts,

Which will increase with other gifts.
Wish what thou wilt, thou shalt it have;
And for to vex both fool and knave,
Thou hast the power to change thy shape,
To horse, to hog, to dog, to ape.
Transformed thus, by any means
Seen none thou harm'st but knaves and queens;
But love thou those that honest be,
And help them in necessity.
Do thus, and all the world shall know
The pranks of Robin Good-fellow;
For by that name thou called shalt be
To ages last posterity.
If thou observe my just command,
One day thou shalt see Fairy Land.
This more I give: who tells thy pranks
From those that hear them shall have thanks.

Robin having read this was very joyful, but he longed to know whether he had this power or not, and so he wished for some meat, and it appeared before him. Then he wished for beer and wine and they were provided straight away.

Then because he was weary, he wished for a horse, and he was instantly transformed into a fine horse that leaped nimbly.

Then he wished he was a dog, and then a tree. So he changed from one thing to another, till he was certain that he could change himself to anything he desired.

How Robin Good-fellow helped two lovers and deceived an old man

When walking through a wood one day Robin heard two lovers despairing because they were being stopped from enjoying each other's company by a cruel old lecher, who would not let this loving couple marry.

Robin, pitying them, went to them and said, 'I have heard your complaints, and pity you. If you do as I say, I will see that you shall have your heart's desire, and it will be sooner than you can imagine.'

The maiden was amazed and said, 'Sir, how can that be? My uncle, because I will not give in to his lust, is so strict with me, and makes me work night and day, so that I have no time to speak with my young man, who I love more than anyone.'

'If your work is all that stops you,' said Robin, 'I will see that it is done: don't ask me how, or doubt me, I will do it. Go off with your love, for twenty-four hours and I will free you. In that time you can get married or do what you desire. I love true lovers, honest men, good fellows, good housewives, good meat, good drink, and all things that are good, but nothing that is ill; for my name is Robin Good-fellow, and you shall see that I have power to do what I have promised.'

Presently, Robin Good-fellow turned himself into a horse, and away he ran. The young couple were both amazed, but when they had got over the shock, they decided to make good use of their time, and went to an old friar who presently married them. They paid the friar, and went to enjoy their first night together.

Robin, when he got close to the old man's house, turned himself into the shape of the young maid. He then entered the house and started to do all the work that the maid had to do, but in half the time that anyone else could do it in.

The old man, seeing how fast 'the maid' was doing the work, thought that maybe she was planning to meet someone that night and gave her more work than anyone could do in one night, but Robin did it in a trice.

In the morning, Robin went to the bedside of the two lovers and bid God give them joy, and told them everything was going well, and that by nightfall he would bring them £10 of her uncle's money to start their life together. The couple thanked him, and he, being contented to see their happiness, went on his way, laughing.

Off went Robin to the old man, who was still marvelling at how the work was being done so soon, and he said, 'Sir, something marvellous has happened to me.'

'Good niece, what has happened?' replied the old man.

'Sir, I am ashamed to say but, weary with work, I slept, and dreamed that I consented to that which you have so often desired of me (you know what I mean), and I thought you gave me as a reward £10, and consent to marry that young man that I have loved so long.'

'Did you really dream that? I will make your dream come true, for I will give you my written consent to marry him that you want to, and as for the £10, go into the barn, and I can bring it to you presently if that is what you wish.'

Robin kept silent and headed towards the barn, while the old man took this as consent and made haste to get out his money, and follow 'the maid'.

When he got to the barn, the old man threw the money on the ground, saying, 'This is the most pleasing bargain that ever I have made,' and went to embrace Robin.

Robin changed into a hare and then a hound and then a hawk, whilst the old man tried to chase him. He then took the old man in his arms and carried him to the pond, where he dragged him through the water to cool his hot blood. After this Robin then carried the old man to where the young married couple were, and said, 'Here is your uncle's written consent, and here is the £10 he gave you, and there is your uncle, let him deny it if he can.'

The old man, afraid of being treated even worse by Robin, said that all was true.

'Then am I as good as my word?' said Robin, and went away laughing. The old man knew himself duly punished, and turned his hatred into love and both he and the couple lived happily ever after.

BLACK DOGS, WILL O' THE WYKES AND LANTERN MEN

You may have heard the tales of Black Shuck in Suffolk, particularly the accounts from 1577 of when this black dog 'or the Devil in such a likeness' entered the churches in Bungay and Blythborough and attacked the parishioners.

Well, over the centuries there have been many sightings of ghostly dogs in other counties including Norfolk, Lincolnshire and Cambridgeshire. Such creatures are said to inhabit church-yards, roads, coasts and fens and are believed to have mythological roots such as the giant three-headed dog Cerberus who guarded the entrance to Hades, or Garm the giant hound that guarded the gate of Hel in Norse myth.

Within Cambridgeshire, sightings of black dogs have been recorded at Cambridge (Arbury Road) Parson Drove, Prickwillow,

Witchford, Snailwell, Soham, Upware, Wandlebury, West Wratting, Brandon Creek and on the A605 between Whittlesey and Coates. In recent years, however, people more commonly see large black cats rather than dogs … but this is a book of folk tales and such sightings of cats have not yet entered that realm, so back to dogs.

James Wentworth Day gave a most entertaining account to illustrate the fear of a black dog that haunted the area between Wicken and Burwell. I have edited the account to make it easier to read.

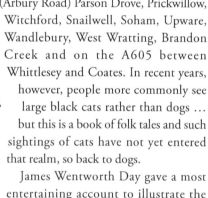

James had been out shooting during the day on Adventurer's Fen and had gone into The Five Miles From Anywhere – No Hurry Inn to share a drink with the 'rough crew of turf-diggers, sedge cutters, and dyke dredgers' and asked if any of the men who sat by the turf fire wanted to join him in taking the shortcut home using the bank rather than the road.

Despite the fact that this route was a mile shorter, none of the men wanted to accompany him, for 'That old black dog run there of nights … if you go, he'll have you as sure as harvest', he was told by one man. Another then added, 'You recollect what happened to one young woman. She up and died after that old dog chased her!'

He tried once more to coax a man to join him but the response once again was, 'You won't catch me on that there bank not tonight nor yet any other night. I wouldn't go there not for the King of England! Ah! You may have that great old gun but if we'd got machine guns and tin hats, I wouldn't go. And if you go, the old dog will have you, sure as harvest.'

More description followed. 'That's the dog. He runs along that bank of nights, big as a calf … black as night, with eyes that glower at you like bike lamps. If he sees you, you'll up and die. There ain't a man living what can see that old dog and live. If he does, he'll go mad.'

James was then informed of how a few years earlier the man's sister had seen the dog whilst she was walking out to meet her sweetheart. 'Big as a calf, sir, he came along that bank quiet as death. Just padded along head down, great old ears flapping. It wasn't more than twenty yards off when it raised its head and glared at her – eyes red as blood. My heart! She did holler. She let out a shriek like an old owl and belted along that there bank like a hare. Run sir! There was nothing that could have caught her … She came bursting along that bank like a racehorse, right slap into her young man. Ha! She did holler. And then, when he grabbed hold of her she went off dead in a faint!'

When James enquired as to the welfare of the girl, he was told that she had not died of fright. He questioned how she had survived the ordeal and was informed, 'It would take more than an old dog to kill her. She's as tough as hog leather. But that wholly laid her up for a week and she's been a complaining about it ever since.'

James Wentworth Day also recorded how, in the Fens, people commonly saw apparitions known as Will o' the Wisps (or Will-o-the-wikes, Willie Wisps, Jenny Lanterns, Jenny-Whisp or Jack o' Lantern). He found them to be either red in colour or looking like ordinary candles. Such phenomena, which we believe now to be caused by the spontaneous combustion of marsh gas, occurred on warm nights in rotten bogs and deep fen pools. The Latin name for this is *ignis fatuus*, meaning 'foolish fire'.

The favourite haunts of such lights were Chatteris, Whittlesey, Peterborough and Thorney. John Clare at Helpston, not far from Peterborough, recorded having seen such an apparition gliding 'onwards as if a man was riding on horseback at full speed with a lanthorn light' and another 'meander lazily towards him in the night-time gloom'. He also noted that he had heard 'the old alewife at The Exeters Arms behind the church often say that she has seen, from one of her chamber windows, as many as fifteen together dancing in and out in a company as if dancing reels'.

Sadly, with the drainage of the fens, meres and marshes, and perhaps with the improved lighting (and even light pollution), the sightings of the 'Will o' the Wisps' have died out.

L.F. Newman, whilst researching the folklore of Cambridgeshire and the Eastern Counties, noted that people in the Fens reported a special form of fire-fiend known as the 'Lantern Man'. He found that sportsmen who were out shooting on the marshes at night never whistled to call their dogs, as they believed that this would call the fiend instead. Should anyone accidentally call up the Lantern Man, the recommended method of protection was 'to lie face downwards on the ground with the mouth buried in mud, so that the apparition will pass over the prostrate body'.

Newman recounted the story of a man who, 'crossing the "medders" at night, whistled to his dog and attracted the notice of a Lantern Man. The whistler fled for shelter into a friend's house, who, in bravado, hung out a horn lantern on a long pole. The Lantern Man hurled himself at the light and it was found next morning with all the horn burnt up as though it had been in a fire.'

The following story is an adaptation of a traditional tale told in the Littleport and Brandon Creek area. It was included by W.H. Barrett in his *Tales from the Fens*, and other collections, though there is some debate over the exact location. I have chosen to set it at Bulldog Bridge, on the A1101 Mildenhall Road close to Shippea Hill and near to the place where Red Mere used to be prior to the extensive draining of the Fens.

THE LEGEND OF BULLDOG BRIDGE

A long time ago, before the Reformation cleared the monasteries and ended the practice of pilgrimages, a causeway across the Fenland was used by pilgrims to get from Thorney Abbey to the Shrine of Our Lady at Walsingham.

This causeway passed a shallow lake known as Red Mere and it was to this place that a young woman was sent from her home in Littleport, to gather wild mint.

It was a warm day in early summer, as the young woman gathered the pungent herb into her apron, and by the time she finished she felt very drowsy.

She found herself a shady spot not far from the roadside, lay down, and was soon fast asleep. But she was not asleep for long before she felt someone tugging at her clothes and bearing down on top of her.

She opened her eyes and saw that an itinerant friar was trying to have his way with her. She cried for him to stop but he threatened to kill her and so, in desperation, she screamed, 'Jesus and Mary save me', and at once a huge black dog came bounding towards her.

The dog flung itself at the friar, tugged his robes and pulled him off the girl. The dog then began tossing the cleric to and fro as if he was a rag doll. In time the dog tired, and the cleric, bleeding profusely, grabbed his knife from his belt and fatally stabbed the dog.

The young woman by this time had fainted, but the wounded dog crawled over to her and licked her hand.

She awoke and saw the man and the dog lying dead beside her. She got up, picked up the mint and hurried home, where she told everyone what had just happened to her.

When they heard her story, the men of Littleport went to the site to retrieve the bodies. They tossed the friar into the mere, making the already red-tinted water even more so. The dog, they gave a decent burial close to the bridge over the river …

However, despite the burial, the dog did not rest and it is said that at dusk on summer nights he can still be seen near Bulldog Bridge.

Another short tale from medieval times but set on the other side of the county is that of the Wild Hunt, which appeared briefly in the area in the twelfth century and seems to have resembled the creatures known collectively as the Nazgul in J.R.R. Tolkien's *Lord of the Rings*.

The *Peterborough Chronicle* records that with the appointment of an abbot, Henry d'Angeley, in 1127, there appeared the following:

> many men both saw and heard a great number of huntsmen hunting. The huntsmen were black, huge, and hideous, and rode on black horses and on black he-goats, and their hounds were jet black, with eyes like saucers, and horrible. This was seen in the very deer park of the town of Peterborough, and in all the woods that stretch from that same town to Stamford, and in the night the monks heard them sounding and winding their horns ...

3

OF RUMOUR, GOSSIP AND TALL STORIES

This chapter contains the lighter stories from around the county, including some of those tales that may have been told as part of the 'liar's contests' noted by Enid Porter, as explored in the introduction to this book. The chapter starts with an account of Mark Twain's visit to the Fens, as recalled by W.H. Barrett, along with an investigation to assess the truth of the account. This is followed by a Cambridgeshire version of a story that has been found across the world and which dates back to at least the sixteenth century, along with a story that is particularly found in East Anglia. The chapter concludes with a folk tale that is perhaps best known for its inclusion in Chaucer's *Canterbury Tales*, along with a couple of old tales from Cambridge University.

I had intended to include a tale of Robin Hood in this chapter, as his persona as the Earl of Huntingdon brings him within the geographical area. However, whilst the names of the legendary 'Hooded Man' along with Little John have been given to two stones, which are nicked in their tops with markings like arrows, in Nene Park (Ferry Meadows), they are more likely to be markers connected to the transporting of Barnack stone to Bury St Edmunds across Gunwade Ferry. The markings recall the fact that St Edmund was killed by arrows.

MARK TWAIN AND TALL STORIES OF THE FENS

Readers of W.H. Barrett's *Tales from the Fens* may have noticed in the introductory chapter, by Enid Porter, a reference to Mark Twain visiting the Fens. The tales recalled by Barrett as being told by the great American writer were not included in Barrett's books but were reproduced in the *Dictionary of British Folk Tales* and *Folktales of England* by Katharine Briggs (the latter in conjunction with Ruth Tongue). Briggs actually recorded the conversation with Mr Barrett in October 1963, but sadly the recordings have disappeared.

Barrett explained how when he was just a child living at Brandon Creek, Mark Twain came there for a visit. He stayed at The Ship Inn, where he heard and told a number of tall tales.

The reason for the visit by Twain, so Barrett was told, was that he was staying at Cambridge whilst recovering from a nervous breakdown, and the fellows of the university, who enjoyed a good tale themselves, thought it would aid his recovery.

Barrett remembered being given sweets by the great American, who always wore a ten-gallon hat. Twain, said Barrett, soon struck a rapport with the old Fenmen, and he also shared their knowledge, experience and love of fishing.

One day Twain informed the Fenmen that, in America, 'the fish were so large that no man could pull 'em out'. Not long after this, Chafer Legge arrived with a team of horses to inform Twain that they were 'waiting for the man that's just going out fishing'!

Another time during Twain's visit, he was shown some large Fenland potatoes by the landlord of The Ship. Twain responded by saying that in his country the spuds were 'so large that we can only get one into a saucepan at a time'.

Later that evening, a big water-tube boiler destined for the Cambridge gasworks was being pulled up the river by a barge. It moored up outside the inn, and Twain asked what it was. The response from the innkeeper was that the boiler was 'one of the saucepans we boil our potatoes in'!

These tall tales are just the sort of stories that Twain was known for, but did he actually stay at Brandon Creek? I wanted to find out.

The historical records show that Mark Twain (whose real name was Samuel L. Clemens) was staying in England in the summer of 1896, when Barrett was just 5 years of age. Clemens and his wife had been travelling around Europe on a lecture tour when they received the news in London that their eldest daughter, Susy, had been taken ill with a fever. Mrs Clemens decided to sail back to America, but shortly after her departure Samuel received the sad news that the girl had died of meningitis. She was just 24 years old and her father had not seen her since he set off on his travels a year earlier.

Clemens, alone in Guildford, Surrey, was distraught. He knew that his wife would not hear about their daughter's demise until the ship docked in New York, and the thought of this was unbearable to him. His way of dealing with the grief was to seek a house in London where he and his family could shut themselves away 'and bar the doors and pull down the blinds …' and he could bury himself in his writing.

For nine months the Clemens family avoided any form of social engagement or publicity. Their daughter Clara was later to recall how her mother was inconsolable, and that the low mood lasted for a couple of years, and it was a long time before anyone laughed in the household. Her father's 'passionate nature expressed itself in thunderous outbursts of bitterness shading into rugged grief'.

It seems unlikely that W.H. Barrett would have made up the story that Mark Twain had visited Brandon Creek. I subscribe to the view that the great American did indeed visit The Ship, where his depression may have been somewhat alleviated by the ready wit of the old fenland storytellers.

It was not just the men at Brandon Creek who could tell a good short story. The talent was found elsewhere in the county but, for some reason, recorded more often in the Fens. Here are a few examples of such tales.

A long time ago, many of the fen droveways were turned into quagmires during the winter. On such an occasion a man met another along one of the droves and he said, 'Have you seen a hat round here?'

'Naw,' said the other man.

'It is not so much the hat that I am worried about, it is the man under the hat, and the horse under him,' replied the first man. 'If I can find the hat, I can find them all!'

Similarly, in Doddington in the mid-nineteenth century, a man was feeling his way around the edge of a newly drained field.

'What on earth are you doing?' said a passer-by.

'I'm looking for my horse. It was here this morning!' replied the man.

Horse-drawn lighters were common on the River Ouse until about 1925. The following story, which is found elsewhere around the country, was told by a man from Wisbech:

> One of the horses that used to draw lighters up the river was blind and had been taught to jump over the stiles whenever the driver shouted, 'Over!' As a result of this, the horse would jump whenever anyone shouted 'Over!'
>
> One day, some of the lighter-men were waiting at a public house at Downham when a man rode up on a hunter, which was famous as a jumper. The owner of the blind horse said to the man, 'I have a horse here that is a better jumper than your hunter.'
>
> The owner of the hunter and the lighter-man made a wager over whose horse was the best jumper and they both led their horses to the road. The lighter-man then laid a piece of straw on the ground, led his horse up to it, and shouted: ' Over!' The horse jumped as high as if it was clearing a stile.
>
> The hunter was then led to the straw and the rider tried to make it jump, but the hunter refused as it could see no obstacle.

Another story collected in the Wisbech area concerns a woman who went to church, leaving her little boy at home to look after the dinner of a sheep's head, some potatoes and an apple dumpling that was cooking in the boiler. Part-way through the church service the boy came running down the aisle and over to his mother. He grabbed her hand and shouted, 'Mother, mother, come home quick.'

The woman said 'sh-sh' to get her son to be quiet.

'I can't, mother,' he said. 'The sheep's head has ate all the taters and the apple dumpling has took off his jacket to fight It.'

The narrator of the sheep's head story explained that all the food was being boiled together and the sheep's jaw had opened and the potatoes had gone into its mouth and the dough had come off the outside of the apple dumpling. The collector believed the story to be a purely local tale.

A short story collected in Chatteris concerns an old man who went into a butcher's shop in wartime. He asked for a sheep's head and the butcher said, 'Do you want me to remove the eyes for you?'

'No,' replied the old man, 'I want it to see me through the week!'

Arthur Dunham of March was not only a very tall man but he was also known for his tall stories. I only wrote the outline of this tale but I hope I do him credit in expanding it.

Jack and his wife were hungry. It was the middle of winter and his wife sent him into the bothy to get some milk from the cow. He put on his coat, hat and wellies and went outside into the cold. Blowing on his hands to warm them, he grabbed the stool and the bucket and set to work.

But the weather was so cold that as soon as the milk came out of the cow it turned to icicles, which he had to break off to put in his bucket. After a few minutes Jack gave up, put a blanket over the cow to keep her warm and went back indoors to stand by the fire to get warm again.

His wife saw this and said to him, 'I don't know what we are going to eat today Jack, there's no food in the house. Do you think you could take the gun and shoot something for us?'

'I'll do better than that,' said Jack, 'I'll go out and catch us a feast. Despite the bad start, I'm feeling lucky today.'

So Jack put on his coat, hat and wellies, took the gun from beside the fire, and went back out into the cold. He hadn't gone far when he saw two birds flying overhead. He quickly aimed, fired and managed to kill both birds with one shot. But the birds fell on the other side of the drainage ditch, and so Jack had to clamber down the bank and then wade through the water to reach them.

When Jack got to the other side of the ditch he found that one of the birds had fallen directly on top of a hare and had killed that too. He picked up the two birds and the hare and carried them back home, but as he reached home he realised that his boots were full of water. He put down his catch and bent down to take off the wellies, only to find that they were full of fish.

So Jack and his wife had a three-course meal that night, and the tale brought Jack more than a couple of pints the next time he went to the pub!

Arthur's tale resembles one told by Fenland storyteller Alan Lamb, in which an old man lying in bed, cold and hungry, shoots down a flock of geese that were flying over his cottage, by firing both barrels of his gun up the chimney!

Versions of the following tale have been found by folk tale collectors across the world. Though it was never included in the definitive Aarne–Thompson folk tale index, Herbert Halpert and Gerald Thomas located forty different versions and found that the story dates back to at least 1566 in France. Within the UK, variants of the story have been collected in England, Scotland, Wales and the Isle of Man as well as in Ireland.

The tale I include here is based on a combination of the story recalled by Jack Barrett as being popular in the pubs around Brandon Creek, and a version told by a retired Great Eastern

Railway guard whose boyhood had been spent in Cambridgeshire, to Mr E.W. Paddick of Hoddesdon who relocated it within Hertfordshire. I have also included a rhyme in the letter, which was found in many versions of the tale.

Two Fat Geese

> *Here are two fat geese fallen out together,*
> *If you'll pluck one, I'll pluck the other,*
> *And make 'em agree like brother and brother.*

There lived once, not far from Ely, two old farmers who farmed next to each other, got married at the same time and had sons of the same age. Being good chapel-going men they named their sons Alpha and Omega, but over time the boys acquired the nicknames Start and Finish.

So it was that the years passed and the boys became men, and the parents died and the sons farmed the land themselves. Well, the two men used to chat to each other over the fence that divided their land, and often used to call round to see each other for a cup of tea.

One day Finish was outside his back door looking at the large tub in which he collected the swill for feeding the pigs, thinking that he ought to get round to emptying it. As he bent over, one of his goats, a large billy, watching from a distance, decided to charge across the yard and deal his owner a blow such that he fell head first into the stinking swill tub.

Having done the deed, the billy goat glanced at his master briefly, lifted up his head calmly, and then walked off into the spinney to the rear of the house.

As Finish lifted his head out of the tub, Start just happened to arrive near the back door carrying under his arm a long piece of wood. He saw Finish, pulling pieces of cabbage leaves and potato peel out of his hair and could not stop himself from laughing.

Finish, not realising that it was the goat that caused his predicament, blamed his friend and, despite Start trying to explain (in amongst laughing), Finish refused to believe him and walked indoors swearing revenge.

The next day happened to be market day in Ely, and Finish took the opportunity to go to visit his lawyer. He explained to the lawyer that he wanted to get compensation from his neighbour for assault and battery. The lawyer agreed to take on the case, assuring Finish that he would win.

Later that day, on hearing that Finish was telling everyone about the assault, Start went to see the same lawyer to bring a case of defamation of character. The lawyer explained that he had agreed to represent Finish and could not work for both of them. He said that he had a friend who was also a good lawyer who may be happy to represent him and that he would give Start a letter by way of introduction.

The lawyer than scribbled a few lines on a piece of paper, folded it and carefully added his seal. Then he handed the letter to Start, who went off to visit the other lawyer. However, by this time Start was feeling quite thirsty and so decided to go for a drink first.

Calling in at The Lamb, Start sat down in his usual seat by the fire and drank a pint of beer, followed by another and yet another.

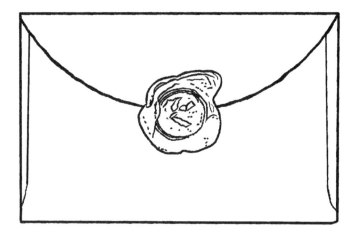

After a while he noticed that the seal on the flap of the envelope was coming loose in the heat and he decided to have a peek inside.

He was astonished to read the following rhyme:

> *Here are two fat geese fallen out together,*
> *If you'll pluck one, I'll pluck the other,*
> *And make 'em agree like brother and brother.*

Start immediately saw what the lawyers were intending to do, and so he went to see Finish, who was having his customary end-of-market-day drink at The Sun, and showed him the letter.

The two immediately shook hands and, over another pint or two, agreed to get revenge on the lawyers for trying to make fools of them.

It just so happened that it was Michaelmas time and there were many geese for sale. Finish brought two fat geese, one of which he gave to his friend, saying, 'You pluck this and save all the feathers.'

Start did this and the following week both men carried two sacks full of feathers to Ely market. They went to the lawyer's office and as they climbed the stairs they spilt the feathers as they went. They reached the landing, still spilling feathers everywhere, then went back down the stairs and returned to The Lamb for dinner and a drink.

When the lawyer returned from his dinner he saw the feathers all over the stairs and the landing and was furious. When he opened his office door the draught from the windows caught the feathers and blew them this way and that, including out of the window and down onto a fishmonger's stall in the market. The fishmonger was not best pleased to find his fish covered in feathers rather than scales, and he called for the local constable.

In time the constable called on the two farmers, who were by this time good friends again, and gave them each a summons to appear before the magistrate's court on charges of causing a breach of the peace.

The two men arrived in court on the appointed day to find that one of the lawyers in the court was the man to whom the letter had been addressed. In their defence Start and Finish said that they had heard that the lawyer had a part-time job plucking geese.

When the magistrate asked what they meant by saying that, Finish produced the letter, which was read before the court:

> *Here are two fat geese fallen out together,*
> *If you'll pluck one, I'll pluck the other,*
> *And make 'em agree like brother and brother.*

After much laughter, the case was dismissed and Start and Finish left the court to go and have a few celebratory drinks!

In the Fenland town of March, there seems to have been a factual incident, within living memory, that resembles the above tale.

Apparently a couple of wealthy farmers from the Manea area had a dispute over the drainage ditch that provided the boundary between their land. It was customary in the area for each landowner to maintain their own side of the ditch, but these two had never done this; instead they kept both sides clear for a distance each.

Both farmers went to see their usual solicitor in the town, only to be told by the managing clerk that the solicitor could not act for both parties. However, the clerk offered a letter of introduction to a solicitor in Peterborough, who could represent the other party.

So, one of the farmers took the letter and set off with his wife to drive to Peterborough, a distance of about twenty miles.

His wife sat in the passenger seat and, in her nervousness, she kept turning over the sealed letter in her hand. By the time the couple had reached Thorney, the envelope had come unsealed and out of curiosity she opened it.

Inside was a brief note, saying, 'I have two fat chickens to pluck, one for you and one for me!'

Reading the note enabled the farmer to see that the only people who would benefit from the dispute were the solicitors. He turned his car round, returned home and reached an amicable settlement with his neighbour.

The following story seems to have originally been collected by the antiquarian Walter Rye in Norfolk; however, Enid Porter recalled hearing a similar story in 1970, set in an unnamed Cambridgeshire village. The Eastern Counties Folklore Society also recorded a short variant from Balsham, which I relate at the end of this piece. I have set the story in Chatteris, a Fenland market town twelve miles north-west of Ely, as a crucial part of the story is the 'bone house' – a room where the bones of the dead were once kept. Such a room may also have been known as a charnel house, catacomb, crypt or ossuary, and these are rare in this country, but some were built at the parish church of St Peter and St Paul in Chatteris.

In 1855 about twenty vaulted box catacombs were built adjoining the south wall of the churchyard on the instructions of the Revd M.A. Gathercole, the local vicar. At that time, the churchyard was full, and closed to new burials. A new cemetery was opened along New Road but Gathercole, it was said, could not bear the thought of his parishioners, or indeed himself, being buried in the same place as nonconformists.

Most of the structure has been demolished, but evidence of eight vaulted catacombs survive, close to Gathercole's memorial stone.

The Fearless Girl

There once was a girl called Mary, and she was fearless; nothing scared her. Her father was a farmer and he had two good friends, a blacksmith and a miller, and they used to meet once a week at least, for a game of cards.

One night as they played cards, they realised that their jug of ale was nearly empty, and they also realised that it was getting late.

But the farmer did not want them to interrupt their game so he called for his daughter and said, 'Mary, will you go down to the inn and fill up the jug of ale?'

His daughter answered, 'I will father.' So the farmer gave her some coins and off she went.

The blacksmith and the miller were amazed at the girl going out on a dark night on her own, and said as much to the farmer.

'She's afraid of nothing,' said the farmer.

The blacksmith, who never missed a chance to gamble, said, 'I bet we can make her afraid.'

'I bet you can't,' said the farmer. 'There's nothing she's afraid of.'

The miller said, 'I bet you a guinea that I can make her afraid, that I can find something that she won't do.'

The blacksmith agreed and it was decided that the following week, when they next got together, they would set Mary a task.

A few days later, the blacksmith went to have a word with the vicar and borrowed the keys to the church; he asked the sexton, who digs the graves and so should not be scared of old bones, if he would hide in the bone house just before midnight and try to scare off the fearless girl, because she needed to be taught a lesson.

The sexton was unwilling at first, but when he was offered half a guinea for his trouble, he agreed.

Well, it so happened that the next cards night was on the night of the full moon.

The farmer, the miller and the blacksmith all gathered together and played cards as usual. As the evening wore on, the farmer said to his friends, 'I thought you were going to have a task for my daughter to do.'

'Aye, there is,' replied the blacksmith. 'Call your daughter in and we'll ask her.'

So the farmer called Mary and when she came into the room the blacksmith said, 'I hear that there is nothing you won't do, is that right Mary?'

'Aye, it is, they say I am fearless,' said Mary.

'I've bet your father that you won't be able to go down to the catacombs of the church, the place where they store the old bones, at midnight, and bring me out a skull.'

Mary said, 'I have no problem with that, I'll do it,' and went back to her chores.

At just before midnight Mary set off; the blacksmith and the miller looked at each other and thought of the money they would share later.

Mary went down to the bone house and opened the door. She reached in and pulled out a skull. As she did so, the sexton called out in an eerie voice, 'Don't touch that, that's my mother.'

The fearless girl put the skull down and picked up another. 'Don't touch that, that's my father,' called the eerie voice.

Mary reached for yet another skull. 'Don't touch that, that's my sister,' called the voice.

The girl shouted, 'Mother, father, sister, brother, I will have a skull and that's the end of it.'

She then hurried out of the bone house and slammed the door firmly shut behind her. At once there was an ear-piercing scream, but Mary carried on walking back home.

When Mary got back to the house with the skull, the farmer, the blacksmith and the miller were waiting for her. 'You've got it then?' said the blacksmith.

'Of course I have,' said Mary, 'I'm fearless.'

'I told you she was fearless,' said her father.

'Tell us all what happened then,' said the blacksmith.

'Well,' said Mary, 'I went into the bone house and grabbed a skull, and a ghost called out "That's my mother", so I grabbed another, and another ghost called out "That's my father", so I grabbed a third and yet another ghost called "That's my sister", but I just grabbed the skull anyway, and went out and slammed the door, and as I walked away I heard a ghost screaming and hollering, but here I am, and here's the skull.'

Well, the blacksmith and the miller said goodnight and they went down to the bone house. They took a flaming torch with them, even though it was the night of the full moon, and when they got there, they carefully opened the door and shone the torch inside.

All was quiet in the bone house, but on the floor they found the sexton, surrounded by skulls and bones. He lay face down – and was stone, cold dead. He had died of fright!

The Balsham dare

One hundred years ago a party was enjoying themselves at a village pub, when the merry conversation turned to wagers on feats of daring. One dared a pal to enter a newly dug grave, remove a skull and bring it to them.

The pal agreed to do this the next evening but, before his arrival, one of the company hid between two graves. The strong-nerved man climbed down into the grave and, as he secured a bone, a voice growled, 'Drop that, that's mine'.

The searcher never turned a hair and searched for another bone, and the hidden man growled 'That's mine'.

At this, the searcher exclaimed, 'Damn it, that's a lie, you never had two skulls.' He won the wager.

I am including the following tale, which is found in Geoffrey Chaucer's *Canterbury Tales* as 'The Reeve's Tale', as the story was at one time a very popular folk tale across Europe, and it is set in Trumpington, a village two miles south of Cambridge.

Also known as the 'cradle-trick' the tale may have been located in Cambridgeshire to provide Chaucer, who was very closely linked to Oxford, with the opportunity to mock the scholars of Cambridge. King's Hall, the college mentioned in the tale, was later to become a part of Trinity College. A similar tale was also included by Boccaccio in *The Decameron*, Day IX tale 6.

The Clerk's Revenge

At Trumpington there was once a mill by a brook, and living within it there was a proud miller who no one dared argue with. He was a thief of grain and meal but no one confronted him with this as he had a dagger of Sheffield steel and it was said that he was not at all afraid to use it!

Simon, despite being plump with a round face, bald head and pug nose, had married well to the pretty (though illegitimate) daughter of the parson, a woman who he watched like a hawk and to whom no other man dared speak.

The couple had two children, a 20-year-old daughter and a baby boy. The daughter was pretty, with broad hips and round breasts and her grandfather, the parson, intended to find her a good husband and make her his heir.

The miller was well connected and handled most of the milling for the college known as King's Hall. He extracted a great toll for the wheat that he ground, and when the steward of the college was ill, and like to die, he started to openly steal from the college.

Two young headstrong clerks from the college, on hearing of the deceitfulness of the miller, decided to go and see for themselves how the thefts were carried out. They were granted permission and the two of them, named John and Alan, loaded a horse with a sack of corn and set off for the mill.

On reaching their destination they explained to the miller how the steward was so ill and that they had brought some corn for him to grind. The miller asked what they planned to do while the corn was being milled and they told him they would like to watch.

Despite this request, the miller was still determined to outwit them. He sneaked off and unbridled their horse and encouraged it to run towards the marshes, where wild mares were running free.

When they had been given the ground corn, the two clerks went to fetch the horse to carry the load back to Cambridge, but they found that the horse had gone. They called out in despair until the miller's wife told them she had seen the horse running off towards the marsh to join the wild mares.

While the two young men ran towards the marsh, leaving the bag of flour behind, the miller took half a bushel out of the sack and told his wife to make it into a loaf.

Eventually, the clerks managed to catch their horse and return to the mill, where they found the miller sitting by the fire. It was after dark and so they begged him to give them lodging for the night and food, in return for payment, as they would not get back to the college before the curfew.

The miller agreed to grant the young men hospitality and sent his daughter for ale and roasted a goose for them. He also secured their horse and made a bed for them in his own chamber, which was also the same room in which his daughter and baby son slept.

The miller and his guests supped and talked and amused themselves through the evening. In time, the miller and his wife retired to bed, placing the cradle at the foot of the bed so that the baby could be rocked and nursed if it woke in the night.

At about midnight Alan, John and the miller's daughter also retired to bed, where the two clerks found the miller and his wife snoring loudly. They soon found that the daughter was similarly noisy.

Realising that they were unlikely to get much sleep that night, Alan theorised that if he could sleep with the young woman this might compensate for the inconvenience they had suffered.

John warned Alan of the risk he was taking, for if the miller found out he would punish them both, but it did not stop Alan from climbing out of his bed and in beside the young maiden. Though she had been sleeping soundly, when she felt Alan beside her she soon roused herself and they 'became one', so to speak.

John, feeling envious of his friend, hatched a plan to make his night more entertaining, and moved the cradle to the foot of his own bed. Shortly after this, the miller's wife woke up, went to pee and returned to check on the baby. Finding the cradle at the foot of the clerk's bed she climbed in with him, thinking it was with her husband.

The young clerk soon leapt up and laid on the wife and gave her a good time, whilst his friend continued to pleasure the daughter. On the third cock crow, Alan got up and said farewell to the girl, who told him that when he leaves the mill he should go to look behind the door where he will find a loaf made from his own meal.

The clerk then groped around to find the bed where his friend should have been lying, but found the cradle there instead. Thinking this was the miller's bed he went to where the miller was actually lying and crept in beside him, saying, 'John, wake up and listen to me. I have coupled three times with the miller's daughter while you have lain here afraid.'

The miller jumped up and grabbed Alan by the throat. Alan fought back and in their struggle the miller fell onto his wife in the other bed. She screamed and said, 'Wake up, husband, the two clerks are fighting!'

John jumped out of bed and groped around to find his staff, which was soon grabbed by the miller's wife who, thinking she was striking the students, hit her husband on the head. He collapsed to the ground and the clerks started to beat him too.

While the miller was recovering from the beating, the two young men dressed and went to load their horse with the meal and the loaf that had been placed behind the door.

They rode back to Cambridge knowing that they had got their revenge upon the corrupt and evil miller, and also had fun in the process.

Thus is the proud miller well beat,
And has lost the grinding of the wheat,
And paid for the supper there as well,
Of Alan and of John that beat him well;
His wife is had, and his daughter else.
Lo, what comes of being a miller false.

Another source of humorous tales based around Cambridge University is *The Facetiae Cantabrigienses* (1825). Within this book can be found the following two tales:

The metamorphosis

A group of Cambridge undergraduates were walking through the city one day, with time to spare and with the desire for some amusement. They saw a donkey tied to a door and, realising that

the owner was probably inside enjoying a pipe and a pint after selling his wares at the market, they decided to play a trick on him.

One of the students said to the others, 'Take the panniers off the donkey and put them on my back and then put the bridle on my head, and then take the donkey well away from here.'

His friends did as he requested and, after a short while, the trader finished his pipe and pint and came out to the street. He was most amazed to see, in place of his donkey, the young man standing with the panniers on his back and the bridle on his head. The student immediately said to the tradesman, 'You must know, sir, that I quarrelled with my father about seven years since, and, for my disobedience, I was changed into the degrading shape of an ass. Since then I have had to endure every hardship, but now you are bound to set me free.'

The trader, fully believing the tale, took off the panniers and bridle, and set the scholar loose.

A few days later, the same tradesman went to a neighbouring country fair to purchase a new donkey, to replace the one he had lost. After viewing different beasts, to his surprise, his old identical ass was offered to him.

On seeing its master, the donkey brayed most piteously to get his attention. But the man would not acknowledge the noise and moved on to the next beast, exclaiming, 'So you have quarrelled with your father again, have you? But darn me if I'll have you again!'

A delicate morsel

A student of Cambridge, who preferred the sports of the field to strutting about the streets of the university town, had been out very early one morning at a fox chase. As he made his way back he was extremely hungry and so resolved to beg for a meal from the first farmhouse he came to.

His sight rendered keener by the hunger pangs of his belly, he soon saw a small house some distance away and, on reaching it, he humbly asked the old lady who answered the door if he might beg some food.

The old woman obliged, saying that all she had to offer was some meat pie, the remains of their meal from the previous night.

'Anything is better than nothing,' cried the student, indicating that he would like her to place the food in front of him immediately, such was his hunger.

'Here it is,' said the woman, producing the pie from the larder just behind the student, who turned around as she spoke. 'Here it is, sir; it is only made of the odds and ends, but I hope you like it, though it has mutton and beef and all sorts in it.'

'Charming! My good woman, you need not apologise; I have never tasted a more delicious pie in my life!' continued the student, as he devoured mouthful after mouthful.

'But there is fish in it, too,' said he, as he greedily sucked what he supposed to be a bone.

'Fish,' exclaimed the old woman, looking intently on what the student had in his hand. 'Fish, no, sir, – oh, my word, if that isn't our Billy's lost comb!'

4

Of Witchcraft
and Murder

This is perhaps the darkest chapter of the book with regards to the subject matter. The first tale is the true tale of a couple and their daughter who were hung for witchcraft in the late sixteenth century. This is followed by some of the accounts of the visit to the county by the self-styled 'Witch-finder General' about five decades later. Next is a dark tale of a murder and a haunting that became the subject of a popular ballad, along with some of the tales connected to Caxton Gibbet, and a particularly gruesome tale from the St Neots area.

The Witches of Warboys

On 5 April 1593, a witchcraft trial took place at the Court Hall, in the marketplace of Huntingdon. Two days later Alice Samuel, her daughter Agnes and husband John, having been found guilty, were hanged on the gibbet at nearby Mill Common. Sir Henry Cromwell, the lord of the manor, received £40 from the sale of the Samuels' property, which he bequeathed for a sermon to be preached on the evils of witchcraft every Lady Day (25 March) by a Doctor of Divinity from Cambridge.

This case occurred over fifty years before the 'Witch-finder General' Matthew Hopkins carried out his campaign of terror in East Anglia. It also became the subject of a pamphlet that outlined how Alice was accused of 'bewitching' the five daughters of her neighbours, the wealthy Throckmorton family, and of causing the death of Lady Cromwell, the wife of Sir Henry.

The whole saga started in November 1589, two months after the Throckmorton family moved to the manor house in Warboys, seven miles north-east of Huntingdon, when their 9-year-old daughter Jane became ill. Their neighbours on the north side were the Samuel family – Alice, John and their unmarried daughter Agnes.

Shortly after the Throckmorton family moved into the manor house, Jane started convulsing so much that she had to be tied to the bed, and she claimed that a cat was ripping the skin from her face. She also had the sensation of insects crawling beneath the skin, and her body went into spasms so dramatic that her head almost touched her heels. Her father, believing that she must have the 'palsy', or epilepsy as we know it today, called the doctor, but after examining the girl and getting her urine tested three times, he declared that it was not the 'palsy' but that the child must be bewitched.

As was the custom of the time, Alice Samuel, their neighbour, visited to enquire after the sick girl and sat herself by the fire, where she took off her black cap. The child, between fits, had pointed at Alice and cried, 'Did you ever see one more like a witch than she is take off her black cap? For I cannot abide to look on her.'

Within a month of the visit by Alice, Elizabeth (age 14) and Mary (age 11) started to exhibit symptoms similar to their younger sister. When the girls saw Alice they too made accusations, 'Take her away – look where she stands here before us … it is she …that hath bewitched us and she will kill us if you do not take her away.'

The Throckmortons, whilst concerned about the accusations by their daughters, could not at this time contemplate the possibility of witchcraft, as they knew that neither they nor their daughters had done anything to upset either Alice Samuel or anyone else in the neighbourhood. However, within a short space of time Grace, the youngest daughter, and Joan, the eldest, also exhibited the same symptoms.

Joan not only accused Alice of bewitching her and her sisters, but also said that Alice intended to attack the other women and servants in the house. The records indicate that this began to happen and the servants, like the children, began to call for Alice to be taken away and burnt, 'for she will kill us all if you let her alone'.

With the cause identified as witchcraft, the Throckmortons began to look for ways to get the culprit to cease their actions. A popular way of doing this was to allow the victim to scratch the witch and, consequently, on St Valentine's eve 1590 Gilbert Pickering, the girls' uncle, went with others to get Alice from her house for a scratching test by Jane. The test was carried out, but it did not prove the counter-charm that was expected.

The next day Elizabeth was taken away by Mr Pickering to his home in Northamptonshire, where her fits continued and other strange behaviour was seen, including playing with her food and walking in a strange manner. The girl also started seeing visions of Alice '… in a white sheet with a black child sitting on her shoulders which makes her tremble all over ...' Unable to cure the girl, Mr Pickering sent her back to Warboys.

Soon after this, Lady Susan Cromwell, wife of Sir Henry Cromwell, as lady of the manor visited the family and was shocked to see the girls falling into their fits. She then summoned Alice to speak with her. The old woman dared not refuse as she was a tenant of the Cromwells.

Lady Susan charged Alice with witchcraft, which the old lady denied. She then cut off a lock of her hair and took some of her hair lace, and gave it to the Throckmortons to burn. We have no accurate record of the conversation, but it is alleged that Alice said to her, 'Why are you afraid of me for I have never harmed you yet?' With these words Alice as much as signed her own death warrant. Lady Cromwell went home that night and experienced terrible dreams, during which she believed that a cat was trying to kill her. She continued to experience bad dreams and her health declined until she died just over a year later.

At Christmas 1590, with the girls still showing symptoms of bewitchment, Mr Pickering and two scholars from Cambridge went to talk to Alice. They found her returning from visiting a neighbour's house and questioned her about her actions.

Alice was very loud in her answers and said that the Throckmorton children were wanton in their behaviour, and that they should be punished. Mr Pickering told Alice that if she had brought wickedness on the children he wished to see her burnt at the stake – he would bring wood and fire to it and get the children to blow the coals. Alice replied that she would wish to see him doused in the pond.

Time passed and the girls afflictions continued, though the elder sisters were much more affected than their younger sisters. But then the nature of the afflictions began to change. On All Hallows eve 1592, the girls stayed at Alice's house and they were fine and ate well (their father provided food), but soon after this Alice became a virtual prisoner in the Throckmorton house. If she dared to go home the girls would convulse and scream as if they were possessed, yet if she stayed with them they were fine.

Eventually the stress became too much for Alice and she began to feel that she had a growth in her belly, as if her stomach was filled with the Devil's spawn, and that consequently she must be a witch and the cause of the dreadful things that had happened.

When Alice grazed her skin, drawing blood, the girls accused her of allowing evil spirits to feed on her blood and demanded she admit that she was a witch. The girls also started talking about how all would be well after the Tuesday following 6 January, the date of the next assizes in Huntingdon.

On Christmas Eve 1592, after the girls begged Alice to let them enjoy Christmas without being possessed, the exhausted Alice finally confessed to them that she believed that she was a witch, and that she must have sold her soul to the Devil. The Throckmortons informed the vicar, who preached a sermon and witnessed a public confession. Alice was then allowed to go home.

John Samuel, her husband, and Agnes, her daughter, when they heard of her confession began to fear for her life and begged her to recant, for they knew that though she was a poor, simple old woman she was not a witch.

By the next morning, when Alice had been refreshed by sleeping in her own home, she had come to agree with her family and denied the confession. For this, the whole family were implicated and on 26 December Alice and her daughter were taken to Buckden to appear before the Bishop of Lincoln. On 30 December the bishop was joined by the justices who persuaded Alice to confess that she had let chickens suck her blood. Eventually she provided names for the demons – Smack, Catch, White and Pluck. Alice, Agnes and John were then committed to Huntingdon gaol to await the next sessions day – Tuesday 9 January, the date that the girls had predicted.

But now Mr Throckmorton started to wonder whether Agnes Samuel had been working with her mother to cause the girls harm. He requested that the girl be released on bail and allowed to stay in his house with his family. Joan returned from her uncle's house and started to make fantastical accusations against Agnes. She said that she could see the demons used by the Samuels and was given

their names. The girl also added the accusation of causing Lady
Cromwell's death and bewitching Mistress Pickering too.

The torment for Agnes became much like that experienced by
her mother. After a few months, in early March, Mary scratched
Agnes violently and then prayed excessively, and shortly after this
she seemed to stop having fits.

A couple of weeks later, Elizabeth accused Agnes and her family
of bewitching her and her sisters, saying, 'Thy mother is a witch,
thy father is a witch, and though art a witch; of all three thou art
the worst.'

John Samuel, who had called round to see his daughter, was then
drawn into the situation. He was repeatedly commanded to say, 'As
I am a witch and consenting to the death of Lady Cromwell so I
charge the spirit to depart from Mistress Elizabeth Throckmorton
and suffer her to be well.' Believing that he would never be allowed
to go home unless he said the words, he dutifully did so, thereby
sealing his fate. He then went home and the girls went to bed.
Elizabeth apparently remembered nothing of what had happened.

Joan's fits reached a climax on Lady Day, 25 March, when she
scratched Agnes until the blood flowed freely. She then asked for
shears to cut her nails so the clippings could be burnt as they had the
blood of Agnes on them. All her sisters proceeded to do the same.

On 4 April 1593, Agnes was taken to Huntingdon to join
her mother for the trial. The following day, at least 500 people
watched the proceedings in the court house. Three indict-
ments were read before the inquest in which John, Alice and
Agnes Samuel were accused of 'bewitching unto death the Lady
Cromwell, late wife of Sir Henry Cromwell of Hinchingbrooke
… and for bewitching Mistress Joan Throckmorton, Mistress
Jane Throckmorton and others …'

The reading of the evidence took from 8 a.m. until 1 p.m., and
during these five hours even more allegations were thrown at the
Samuels. John Samuel at first refused to speak, until Judge Fenner
threatened him with immediate execution. Alice and Agnes
bravely accepted their fate. Upon hearing the Samuels' oaths,

the Throckmorton children immediately became well. With the admissions of guilt by the Samuels, Judge Fenner ordered that they be taken away to be hanged.

In 1911, Wallace Nottestein, assistant professor of history at the University of Minnesota, in his *History of Witchcraft in England from 1558–1718*, noted the similarity between the case of the Throckmorton girls and the witch trials in Salem, Massachusetts, ninety-nine years later. He noted how Alice accused the girls of 'wantonness' and theorised that though there may have been a genuine ailment that afflicted the girl (or girls) in the beginning, the others imitated the behaviour.

But now, more than 400 years later, historians and scientists have come up with another theory as to what first caused the girls to experience such terrible, painful spasms, and it has nothing to do with witchcraft. In 1976 Professor Linda Caporael, of Renssaelar Polytechnic Institute, New York, noticed a link between the strange symptoms reported by the accusers in the Salem witch trials of 1692 and the hallucinogenic effects of drugs like LSD.

LSD is a derivative of ergot, a fungus that affects rye grain. Professor Caporael carried out some more research and found that not only was rye the staple diet for the parts of Salem affected, but the weather conditions were also ideal for ergot. Following the publication of her research, historians began to study demographics, weather, literature and crop records to look for further cases. A link was found between drops in population in communities that had diets of rye bread at times of damp weather. An historian also found links between a large proportion of witchcraft trials in Europe and regions where rye was usually grown.

When the Throckmortons arrived in Warboys, rye had become a staple crop in East Anglia. It is now speculated that the family had eaten bread made with rye containing ergot. Within a short time all five of the sisters were suffering from uncontrollable fits and frightening hallucinations. Whether or not the girls, after the toxins had left their systems, feigned the symptoms to bring about the demise of their old neighbour Alice Samuel is more difficult to determine. It may be, as one historian theorises, that after exaggerating some of the symptoms, the girls felt they dare not admit that they were now well.

Whatever the case, the details of the trial were very quickly published under the title 'The most strange and admirable discoverie of the three Witches of Warboys'.

To my knowledge there is no actual memorial to the Samuel family, though in the village of Warboys, witches are depicted on the village sign, the weather vane above the clock tower and on the kits of the local sports teams.

Warboys Community Primary School logo also includes a witch on a broomstick. The witch image, which has been on the school uniforms for over sixty years, was almost abandoned in 2008 by the school governors due to comments that parents and future teachers might be put off by such a logo. Fortunately, a petition signed by 1,000 local residents – and media coverage that reached Canada, the United States, Sri Lanka and even South Africa – led to it being retained as a part of a new design.

Until recently there used to be a Throckmorton family tombstone in the churchyard at Warboys, and the local children used to 'scoot past' it so that the Devil would not get them. Other children would play a game where they hopped around the tombstone three times, spitting on each of its corners. They would then bend down and put their ear to the stone, for they believed that this would enable them to hear the Devil rattling his chains below.

The Lady Day sermon preaching against witchcraft is believed to have continued in All Saint's Church, Huntingdon until 1814.

The Witch-finders in Cambridgeshire

When Matthew, the fourth son of James Hopkins, the vicar of Great Wenham, Suffolk was born in the timber-framed rectory opposite the church in 1619, Puritanism was dominant in East Anglia, particularly in his family.

James Hopkins had been raised in Littleport, the third son of a gentleman who had made his money by enclosing the common land, and who consequently owned not just land but several houses, crofts and fishing waters. The eldest son, Robert, went to Cambridge University and then took a position instructing the 'godless' in a house of correction. Young James likewise followed a career in the Church.

When Charles II succeeded to the throne in 1630, many believed that the pomp and ceremony of the pre-Reformation church would be reintroduced, and so the most devout chose the path of the pilgrim and sailed to America to practise their faith in the way they believed they should.

One of those who made the Atlantic crossing was Matthew's eldest brother, who was planning to follow his father as a clergyman. Matthew, however, chose a different career. He certainly learned to read and write in English and Latin and may have trained with a lawyer's clerk in Ipswich.

Whatever his training, by the time he reached adulthood Matthew had become, in the words of historian Malcolm Gaskill: 'a physically slight man ... a hothead – edgy, impetuous, devious, but charismatic and persuasive. He was also very energetic, arrogant, and ostentatious in his manner and dress.'

In contrast to the wealth of the gentry, such as the Hopkins family, life for the poor in the seventeenth century had become much more difficult than in earlier centuries. In medieval times every parish had its 'wise' or 'cunning' man or woman whose good deeds more than eclipsed the bad. These 'wise' men and women provided their skills to help the people, through making healing potions, stroking (faith healing) and midwifery, along with dowsing to find lost property, and astrology. The Church also provided assistance for the poor and the sick. The Reformation put an end to all the church provision – instead the belief had grown that people could succumb to the devil to get money, food or other assistance, thus breeding suspicion of the powers of the 'wise' men or women.

Slow lingering illnesses, such as tuberculosis or what we now call cancers, were particularly likely to be blamed on 'witches' – and if a 'wise woman' were somehow involved with the sick person she may well be implicated. Similarly, if a cow or a pig died (and at this time such a loss could prove devastating to the micro-economy of a smallholding), a motive would be looked for such as an old woman not being invited to attend a christening, funeral or harvest supper.

Matthew Hopkins observed the belief of the people that 'if any adversity, grief, sickness, loss of children, corn, cattle, or liberty happen unto them, by and by they exclaim upon witches'. These 'witches' were typically people who had poor reputations, low social status, and perhaps lived alone or distant from the community.

Young Matthew regarded this fear of witches as something that needed to be acted upon, and at a time when most people saw the Civil War as an indicator of a 'world turned upside down' – and when many magistrates were dismissing petty accusations as they had bigger matters to deal with – he soon found a purpose in life.

The campaign of the self-styled Witch-finder General began in Essex in 1645. By autumn 1646 Hopkins, who had been joined by John Stearne, had taken the campaign into the surrounding counties of Suffolk, Bedfordshire, Cambridgeshire, Huntingdonshire, Northamptonshire and Norfolk.

Hopkins was not at all afraid of witches, but he was absolutely appalled and disgusted by the thought that they made pacts with Satan. To him this was seen as a diabolical mirror image of the very covenant that good Protestants would form with Christ, and it made him determined not only to convict witches, but also to put pressure on them to reveal the networks of other witches that he believed must exist.

Since self-incrimination was discouraged under English law, Hopkins and Stearne aimed to show that the witches were receiving 'visits' from the Devil's 'familiars' or 'imps' (animals or insects) who suckled from 'teats' found on their body. The 'searchers' (usually women, but sometimes men) would then examine the suspect looking for polyps, warts, haemorrhoids, spots or pimples, which were all potential 'teats'. To get confessions he kept the accused tied to a stool and without food or sleep until they satisfactorily answered his leading questions and implicated others.

For about eighteen months, Hopkins and Stearne worked unhindered, earning up to twenty shillings for each 'witch' who was found guilty. This was a huge amount, which Hopkins defended by saying that finding witches required great skill and courage.

In Huntingdonshire the witch-finders accused as many as twenty witches, and examined more than ten. From this at least five witches were convicted. At the trial in April 1646, the recorder was John Davenport, who sorted the testimonies and details of the trial to be published in a pamphlet. This document provides an amazing glimpse into the mindset of the people of the time, and I would like to provide you, below, with the stories behind two of these confessions.

The case of Elizabeth Chandler

Elizabeth Chandler of Keyston was a widow. About two years before the arrival of the witch-finders she had been harshly treated by Mary Darnell, the wife of William, the village blacksmith, who called her a common scold and caused her to be ducked in the village pond.

As a consequence, Elizabeth wished to see revenge on goodwife Darnell and, six months later, Elizabeth was troubled with visits by the 'roaring' things. She confessed that something had visited her five times, in a puffing and roaring manner: the last visit had been a week before her trial. After the thing left her she felt sore in her body, especially around her belly, and she prayed for deliverance.

There were two main accusations against Elizabeth, both dated back to about a year before the witch-finder's arrival. On the first occasion 9-year-old Katherine Darnell was eating frumity (spiced wheat porridge) with another child brought up by Elizabeth Chandler. The two children started to argue and when Katherine went home she told her mother that goodwife Chandler had given her a 'box of the ears'.

Young Katherine complained of a pain in that ear until she died three weeks later, and during the time that she was ill she often squealed and screeched out that goodwife Chandler had come to her and would kill her.

Elizabeth denied sending a spirit to harm her or using any means to spoil the Darnell family, but Mary had more evidence. She said that, also about a year earlier, she had made some frumity and had invited neighbours to the house to enjoy it with her. But when she took the frumity off the fire it continued boiling for an hour and she could not stop it from boiling over, although she put it into great bowls, tubs and other large vessels. Mary believed that the frumity had been spoiled by Beelzebub, at the instigation of goodwife Chandler.

The case of John Winnick

John Winnick, a labourer of Molesworth, testified that about twenty-nine years earlier, he being a bachelor, lived at Thrapston where he was employed by Buteman, a husbandman and landlord of The George Inn.

While John was a servant of Buteman, he lost a purse with seven shillings in it (about two weeks' wages) and he suspected that one of Buteman's family had stolen it.

John recalled how, one day, he was in the barn at about noon, making hay bottles for his horses, and was swearing, cursing, raging and wishing to himself that some wise body (or wizard) would help him to find his purse and money again.

At once there appeared in front of him a spirit, black and shaggy, with paws like a bear, but about the size of a rabbit. This spirit asked John why he was so sorrowful, and he said that he had lost his purse and money, and did not know how to get it back.

The spirit said to John, 'If you will forsake God and Christ, and fall down and worship me I will help you find your purse and money again.'

John said he would do this and fell down on his knees and held up his hands. The spirit said, 'Tomorrow about this time of day, you shall find your purse upon the floor where you are now making bottles: I will send it to you, and will also come myself.'

The next day at noon, John went into the barn, and found his purse upon the floor. He picked it up, but before he had time to look in it, the spirit appeared to him and said, 'There is your purse and your money in it.' He later found that all the money that was formerly lost was now in the purse.

John knelt down and said, 'My Lord and God I thank you,' and then he saw that the spirit had brought with him two other spirits – one in shape, size and colour like a white cat, and the other like a grey rabbit.

The bear spirit then said to John, 'You must worship these two spirits as you worship me, and take them for your gods also.' John turned his body towards them, and called them his lords and gods.

John was also told that when he died the spirit must have his soul, and John agreed. He also told him that the creatures must suck his body, and to this he also yielded, but they did not suck at that time.

The bear spirit promised him that he would never want for food and drink. He was also told that the cat spirit would hurt cattle when he would desire it and the rabbit-like spirit would hurt men when he desired.

John was then asked to seal the covenant in blood, and the bear spirit leapt onto his shoulder, and pricked him on the head. After taking some blood from him, the three spirits vanished away.

The next day, again at about noon, the three spirits came to him when he was in the field, and told him they had come to suck his body, to which he yielded, and they sucked his body at the places where marks could be seen.

In his testimony, John said that since that time, the three spirits had come to him once every twenty-four hours, sometimes by day, and most commonly by night. When he was asked what mischief he had caused any of the said spirits to do, he answered never any, but admitted that he had sent his bear spirit to provoke the maid-servant of Mr Say of Molesworth to steal victuals for him out of her master's house, which she did.

One of the people who had witnessed the Huntingdon witch-finder trials was John Gaule, the vicar of Great Staughton. When Gaule found that Hopkins was preparing to visit his town, he preached openly against the witch-finder and collected and published evidence of the man's methods and use of torture.

Many of those accused of witchcraft were hanged. Gaule remarked on the actions of Hopkins and Stearne that, 'Every old woman with a wrinkled face, a furred brow, a gobber tooth, a squint eye, a squeaking voice, or a scolding tongue, having a rugged coat on her back, a skull cap on her head, a spindle in her hand and a dog or cat by her side, is not only suspected, but pronounced for a witch.'

However, it was other factors that caused the reign of the witch-finders to end. When the authorities decided that the costs of prosecuting witches should be met by taxpayers, witch-hunting rapidly went out of fashion. Hopkins avoided visiting Great Staughton and, shortly after this, he seemed to have parted company with his colleague and returned home, where he died in

August 1647, probably of consumption, though a poem written in about 1660 included the rumour that he had been lynched.

John Stearne continued the work for a time and, like Hopkins, even wrote a pamphlet explaining and justifying his work. He lived for another twenty years. It was he who supported the investigations of Cambridgeshire witches, the last of which was held in Ely in 1647.

At Sutton, in the Isle of Ely, Stearne interrogated Bridget Bonham, who after being deprived of sleep declared her husband to be a witch. Her 69-year-old husband, John, admitted to cutting his finger to make a pact with a mole-like black creature.

In Stretham, Margaret Moore 'confessed herself guilty' and said she had made a pact with a spirit called Annys, who appeared to her in the shape of a child, along with the spirits of her three dead children. This creature had asked Mrs Moore to make a pact with the Devil to save her remaining sick child. Also in Stretham, Stearne accused a poor couple, Robert and Dorothy Ellis, of witchcraft, along with two other women, Elizabeth Foot and Joan Salter. Dorothy died in jail while awaiting the trial.

At Haddenham, Joan Biggs was released after refusing to confess, as no teats had been found on her body. Also in the village Stearne examined an eccentric, twice widowed, but very religious man named Adam Sabie.

The trials were held in Ely and, on the first day, Chief Justice Godbold led a procession from the cathedral to the Sessions House in the marketplace. At the same time, sixteen defendants (thirteen of whom were accused of witchcraft – eight women and five men) were led in chains from Bishop's Gaol along Market Street to the trial.

The outcome of the proceedings was the acquittal of John and Bridget Bonham, Adam Sabie and Thomas Pye. Margaret Moore was found guilty and hanged along with the convicted criminals.

On a trip through the Fens, Stearne also discovered witches in Chatteris, March, Wimblington and Wisbech. In the latter he interrogated a widow named Joan Pigg who was viewed as being of 'evil fame'. All of these alleged witches arrived too late for the assizes and their eventual fate – along with that of Elizabeth Foot, Joan Salter and Robert Ellis – is not known.

History does not give us exact evidence as to how many people were killed as a result of the actions of the 'witch-finders' but it is believed that up to 300 may have been interrogated, and about one-third of that number hanged.

MATCHAM AND THE DRUMMER BOY

I remember I once heard my grandfather say,
That some sixty years since he was going that way,
When they showed him the spot Where the gibbet was not-
On which Matcham's corpse had been hung up to rot;
It had fallen down but how long before, he'd forgot;

'The Dead Drummer', Ingoldsby Legends

There once stood beside the Great North Road, close to a coppice halfway between Brampton Hut and Alconbury, a tall gaunt post. This post, which was removed in the mid-nineteenth century, had marked the spot where a gibbet had held the mortal remains of Gervase (or Jarvis) Matcham, a man who cruelly murdered a little drummer boy in 1786. This act inspired a number of poems and songs, including one found in the Revd Richard H. Barham's *Ingoldsby Legends.*

Matcham (or Matchan, as it was sometimes written) grew up in Fradlingham in East Yorkshire to middle-class parents. He did not like the pastoral life and so left home at the age of 12 to seek adventure.

First he went to work for Mr Hugh Bethell at Rise Park, as a stable boy or trainee jockey, where he remained for five years. In time he became a horse dealer and was sent by the Duke of Northumberland to deliver a gift of horses to the Emperor of Russia. Whilst on this journey Matcham decided that he would like to become a sailor, and when he returned to England, he joined one of His Majesty's ships as an ordinary seaman, and went on a voyage to the West Indies.

He soon realised that the life at sea was not up to his expectations, so he left the service on his return to England, and attached himself to an infantry regiment. But Matcham discovered that this new regime was also unsuitable for his temperament. He disliked the military discipline, and persuaded a private in the regiment to join him as a deserter when they were stationed at Chatham.

The two men managed to leave the barracks at night and to steal two civilian suits from a nearby gentleman's residence. They then set off walking across the country, and eventually ended up at the horse racing at Portholme near Godmanchester, where they hoped to make some money or gain employment. Whilst there they were almost arrested as deserters, but managed to tell an ingenious tale and gain their release.

With an increased awareness of their dangerous position the men now found it challenging to even get food, and so Matcham decided to re-enlist, this time in the 49th Regiment of Foot, who were recruiting in Huntingdon at the time.

A few weeks after joining the regiment, on 18 August 1780, Matcham was chosen to escort Benjamin Jones, a 15-year-old drummer boy, to Diddington Hall, where they were to collect the regiment's subsistence money. The boy, who was the son of the regiment's Quartermaster Sergeant Jones, was given a bag containing about £7 in gold, and the two set off back to the regiment. However, either intentionally or by mistake, they took the wrong turn and ended up having to stay the night at The White Horse at Alconbury.

It is said that, whilst sharing a drink or two, Matcham hatched a plan to get rid of the boy so that he could keep the bag of money. The next morning the two retraced their steps to Huntingdon and, as they walked, Matcham continued to think that if he could kill the boy, he could take the gold out of the country and start a new life elsewhere.

As Matcham and the drummer boy passed the wood not far from Creamer's Hut (now known as Brampton Hut), he seized the boy and cut his throat. He then seized the bag of gold and fled, travelling back through Alconbury, and then on to Stilton and Wansford, where he purchased a new suit of clothes.

After continuing his journey to Stamford, Matcham picked up the stage coach to York, and then went to visit his mother in Fradlingham, his father having since died. By the time the body of the murdered boy was found some days later, Matcham, was on board a ship and serving again as a sailor in the navy, having fallen victim to the press gang. He fought in several naval engagements, and was discharged in 1786.

Shortly after this, whilst crossing Salisbury plain with a sailor friend, there came a violent thunderstorm and in amongst the crashing thunder and the flashes of lightning Matcham was horrified to see the ghostly figure of the drummer boy standing ahead of him.

His friend was later to describe the spectre as something resembling a deformed woman. He threw a stone at it and it sank into the earth. Both men then became alarmed, and concluded that it was a sign that one of them had offended the divine law, and they must therefore make amends.

In order to determine which of them was the criminal they continued on their journey, walking slightly apart from each other, but they had not gone far when the boundary and milestones on their way started rolling over in front of them. By this time, Matcham was terrified, and beginning to betray his guilty conscience, and so the men looked for somewhere to take refuge for the night.

They found an inn, but before they could enter it Matcham again saw the figure of the drummer boy at the side of the road, standing in his uniform with his drum beside him, and what he believed to be the figure of 'our Saviour' standing on the other.

Eventually, the two men entered the inn, ordered drinks and sat down. But Matcham's companion was still overwhelmed by the recent experience and revealed the details to their companions. Matcham confessed to the murder of the boy six years earlier, and voluntarily surrendered himself to the officers of the law. He was taken before the Mayor of Shrewsbury and was sent for trial at the Huntingdon assizes.

Matcham was convicted and sentenced to death by hanging at Huntingdon on Wednesday, 2 August 1786. After he had been executed, his dead body (wearing the red uniform of his regiment) was ordered to be hung in chains at the spot where the murder was committed, in order that the ghastly spectacle might serve as a warning to prevent similar crimes in future.

Sir Walter Scott, in his *Letters on Demonology and Witchcraft* (1884), gave a different account of the above events, setting them in the West Country and saying that: 'He perpetrated his crime, and changing his dress after the deed was done, made a long walk across the country to an inn on the Portsmouth road, where he halted and went to bed, desiring to be called when the first Portsmouth coach came. The waiter summoned him accordingly, but long after remembered that, when he shook the guest by the shoulder, his first words as he awoke were: "My God! I did not kill him."'

A pamphlet was published detailing Matcham's supposed confession to the Revd J. Nicholson of Great Paxton. Tales were told of how the last gibbet in Huntingdonshire was constructed on the Buckden Road, and maps indicate that the place was known as Matcham's Bridge or Matcham's Gibbet.

Cuthbert Bede (the Revd Edward Bradley) recorded the memories of an old cottager in *Notes & Queries*:

Matchan's body was hung in chains, close by the road side, and the chains clipped the body and went tight round the neck, and the skull remained a long time after the rest of the body had got decayed. There was a swivel on the top of the head, and the body used to turn about with the wind. It often used to frit me as a lad, and I have seen horses frit with it. The coach and carriage people were always on the look out for it, but it was never to my taste. Oh, yes I can remember it rotting away, bit by bit, and the red rags flapping from it. After a while they took it down, and very pleased I were to see the last of it.

After reading the *Ingoldsby Legend* version and that of Scott, Bede went back to his local informant for more information:

It was about a mile from Alconbury, as you go Easton, where it was done. But it was ill-convenient to hang him just at that spot; so they put up the gibbet nigher to Alconbury, on a bit of ground belonging to the parish-clerk, close against the river. The river often flooded over there, so that the coaches and posting-carriages had something to do to get safe over, and the bridge was narrow, so there were white posts set up, painted black on the top. The chains clipped Matcham's body quite close, in the way I told you — close round his head and down his arms and his legs, and he hung by a swivel, and twisted round with the wind, and would blow straight out when there was a hurricane.

The man continued to explain how some 'audacious' drover boys were not frightened of the gibbet:

There was a sight of drovers on the road at that time; and them owdacious drover-boys, instead of being frit at Matcham, used to make game of him. I [remember] one morning when I had to go from 'The Wheat-sheaf' to Easton, betwixt three and four o'clock, just as it were dawning, and, when I got nigh the Gibbet, there was Matcham had been took down — for the swivel had broken — and he was stuck right up on one of the posts. It gave me a turn, I can promise you. It was never rightly found out who did it, but it always were laid on them owdacious drover-boys.

A couple of other tales about the gibbet have been collected in the area. One concerns a group of young men who were drinking in a nearby inn when they got on to the subject of Matcham and speculated that, as it was a cold night, the man on the gibbet might appreciate some hot broth! One of the company offered to take some to him for a wager.

A ladder was fetched, and carried with the broth to the gibbet. However, whilst all this was happening, another young man in the group had gone ahead to hide near the gibbet. When the man had climbed the ladder and was just about to offer the hot broth to the corpse, the trickster called out, 'Cool it, cool it.' This resulted in the terrified lad falling from the ladder and never regaining his sanity.

It is also said that at one time a Huntingdon baker's cart was passing the gibbet and the baker's assistant threw a small bread roll at the body, saying that 'Matcham must be hungry'. The roll struck the skull and got lodged in the mouth.

The *Ingoldsby Legend* also includes some gruesome details of the gibbet:

> *So Justice was sure, though a long time she'd lagged,*
> *And the Sergeant, in spite of his 'Gammon' got 'scragg'd;*
> *And people averr'd that an ugly black bird*
> *The Raven, 'twas hinted, of whom we have heard,*
> *Though the story, I own, appears rather absurd,*
> *Was seen (Gervase Matcham not being interr'd),*
> *To roost all that night on the murderer's gibbet;*
> *An odd thing, if so, and it may be a fib – it,*
> *However's a thing Nature's laws don't prohibit*
> *– Next morning they add, that 'black gentleman' flies out*
> *Having pick'd Matcham's nose off, and gobbled his eyes out!*

There is nothing to be seen today of the gibbet, but it is said to have been situated at the junction where you turn off the A1 northbound carriageway to go west to the village of Woolley.

The previous story mentions gibbeting, and in case you, the reader, would like to know more about this form of punishment I will reveal something of it before moving on to the next tale.

A gibbet was an iron cage that was hung from the wooden arm of a standard hangman's drop. It was erected near the scene of the crime and was used for serious capital offences, including highway robbery and murder.

The criminal would have been hanged in the conventional way and then, after an hour, or when they were pronounced dead, the body, often coated in pitch, would be wrapped in chains or placed in an iron cage. The lifeless corpse would then be left to rot, often for many years, as an example to all of the penalty for such criminal action.

Many folk tales survive that describe the gibbeting of murderers whilst still alive, of how their head was clamped at the top to ensure the maximum discomfort, and how they would either die from starvation, dehydration or exposure. However, researchers have been unable to find any mention of such gruesome punishment in the court or burial records.

The Gruesome History of Caxton Gibbet

Perhaps the most famous gibbet in Cambridgeshire is situated a mile and a half from Caxton, near the junction of Ermine Street (the London to Huntingdon road, now the A1198) and the Oxford to Cambridge Road (A428). There are various folk tales about this gibbet, the most common being from the eighteenth century.

In Monk Field, Bourn, about a mile from Caxton village, a man named Partridge was robbed and cruelly murdered by a man from Yorkshire. The murderer escaped capture and fled to America, but returned after seven years to England and to the site of the dreadful deed.

He spent time in a pub in Caxton where the locals realised that he was not a stranger to the area. They asked him questions, and the drink having loosened his tongue, he made a cryptic comment that he had eluded the gamekeepers after poaching some partridges.

The publican recalled the earlier murder and informed the authorities, who arrested the man. He was tried and sentenced to be hung in the cage and starve to death.

Another variant of the tale concerns a man named Jack (or John) Williamson who had a black lurcher called Flash who accompanied him everywhere. When Flash became ill and died, Williamson blamed a man called Albert Partridge, who he knew envied Flash. Partridge and Williamson got into a fight in which it is said that the former was killed. The latter went drinking and was heard muttering about partridges, and when Albert's body was found he was the prime suspect. For his crime, Williamson was also said to have been gibbeted alive.

It was also said that a baker, passing the gibbet, took pity on Williamson's suffering and offered him a bread roll. It is rumoured that he was hanged for this act of kindness.

The stories of Partridge have been spread widely. However, as is often the case, research has failed to uncover any record that verifies the story in either court or burial records. However, of the gibbet itself, there are some more recent stories that are interesting in their own right.

In 1919 a Cambridge newspaper reported the following:

> Great amusement has been caused among residents in the neighbour-
> hood and hundreds of passers-by at the hanging of the 'Kaiser' from
> the Caxton Gibbet. Here, where, in days gone by, murderers and
> miscreants were said to have been hanged, the 'Mad Dog of Europe'
> is now suspended by the neck. Attached to the effigy, which swings in
> the breeze, is the guilty admission, 'I deserve it — Kaiser Bill.'

In 1934 the gibbet was rebuilt from timbers rescued from the
demolition of an old cottage in Baldock. Five years later, it was
cut down by someone leaving a stump just six inches high. The
'carcass' was carried with 'due solemnity' to the nearby hotel yard,
and the brewery, realising the importance of the landmark, ordered
a replacement.

On 15 October 1946 Reichmarshal Hermann Goering committed suicide, the night before he was to be executed. Two days
later the newspapers reported that a full-size effigy of Goering,
complete with jack boots and medals, was found hanging from
Caxton gibbet.

The gibbet again made the news in 1984, during the miners'
strike, when it was used to hang an effigy of union leader Arthur
Scargill. The effigy was said to have appeared overnight, bearing the
words 'Scargill, Scum of the Earth'. No one claimed responsibility.

Today, visitors to the site can see the replica gibbet near the new
McDonald's restaurant, a short distance from the roundabout that
still carries it's name.

If the following tale is true, the woman would have passed Caxton
gibbet on her eleven-mile journey along the Cambridge Road from
Elsworth to St Neots.

The tale was printed in a book of crimes in 1825, and then
repeated by Saunders in his *Legends of Huntingdonshire* (1888).

Saunders noted its source as the *University Weekly Journal* of 8 March 1740. I have been unable to locate the journal or verify any other details from the account, but as it has all the ingredients of a folk story I have included it within this collection.

The Beastly Butcher of St Neots

A woman living at St Neots, returning from Elsworth where she had been to receive a legacy of £17, hid the money in her hair for fear of being robbed. Before she reached her home, she overtook her next-door neighbour, a butcher by trade, who also kept an inn and lived in fair reputation. She was glad to meet him, told him what she had been about, and where she had concealed her money.

The butcher, finding a convenient opportunity when they reached a lone part of the road, dragged her from her horse, cut her head off and put it into his pack, and rode on as quickly as the horse could carry him.

Directly afterwards, a gentleman and his servant saw the body on the ground. The man ordered the servant to gallop on at all speed and to follow the first man he overtook, wherever he went. The servant caught up with the butcher about a mile ahead and asked what the town was in front of them.

The butcher replied, 'St Neots.'

'My master,' said the servant, 'is just behind, and has sent me forward to enquire for a good inn.' The murderer answered that he kept one of the best in the town, where they should be well entertained.

The gentleman soon caught up with them, and when they reached the house he dismounted and told his man to look after the horses while he took a stroll through the town. He said he would return presently.

Instead of going for a stroll, the gentleman went straight to a constable and related the whole affair. The constable was most surprised as he believed the butcher to be a very honest man, who had lived there many years with an excellent character.

Nevertheless, the constable went back with the gentleman immediately and, searching the butcher's pack he was greatly surprised and shocked when he discovered and recognised the head of his own wife.

The murderer was sent to Huntingdon gaol, tried shortly after, and executed.

5

OF PEOPLE
AND PLACES

In this chapter the stories are closely linked to specific places. The
first explores the tales connected to the hills known as the Gog
Magog Hills. This is followed by a selection of tales concerning
the disappearance of policemen in the county in the nineteenth
century, and some stories and historical detail relating to the plight
of French prisoners during the Napoleonic Wars, who were stationed at Norman Cross. The section ends with an account of the
plight of Elizabeth Woodcock, who was trapped beneath seven feet
of snow in 1799. Her experience is still acknowledged through the
presence of a memorial, which can be seen from the Cambridge
guided busway.

GOG MAGOG AND THE LAND OF THE GIANTS

A few miles south-east of Cambridge, to the north of the A1307
road to Haverhill, are the Gog Magog Hills. The place name
dates back at least to the sixteenth century but its origins are
unclear. Gog, the chief prince of the land of Magog, is referred to
in the Bible (Ezekiel 38–39) as being the instigator of a terrible
battle, and the name also appears in the Qur'an. The names Gog
and Magog are also included in the Bible in the Revelation of

St John, as being enemies of God who will eventually be overcome (20: 7–9).

But who was Gog Magog or Gogmagog? For this we need to go back to ancient times and to a tale found in the medieval chronicles, but which fell out of favour in later centuries.

Long ago in Greece, there lived a king who had thirty daughters of marriageable age. The king and his wife held a great feast to which they invited all the princes and knights from far and wide, in order that they could arrange marriages for the girls. The weddings took place over three days.

It soon became clear that the girls were unhappy with their matches. They believed the men to be beneath them in status, and they jointly determined not to submit to the rule of any man. The husbands complained to the king and he invited his daughters to his court where he reproached them for their behaviour. The sisters, now even more angry, decided to kill their husbands by slitting their throats as they slept.

But the youngest sister quite liked her husband, and confessed to him, and he told the king of the plans. The girls were arrested and imprisoned awaiting trial, but no judge or jury could be found who would sentence the king's daughters. Instead a decision was made that the girls should be set adrift in a rudderless boat so that fate could decide their future.

The boat drifted until it ran aground on the shore of a strange, uninhabited island. The girls alighted and the eldest decided that they should call the island Albion after her, as she was the first to set foot on the land.

The sisters then went in search of food. For the first few days they ate the fruits of the trees until their strength returned. Then, being used to hunting using bow and arrow, hawk and hound, they had to rediscover the old ways of hunting, fishing and trapping, along with lighting fires to cook their food. Whilst out hunting the girls also looked for inhabitants of the land, but found none.

Time passed and it is said that loneliness, and the diet of mainly meat, made the girls long for male company. Devils, which lived in caves, noticed this, turned themselves into men, and lay with the sisters. And so Albion became populated by a race of giants that spread out across the land.

The giants, not surprisingly given their origins, were always fighting. Many years later when Brutus, the great-grandson of Aeneas, came to Albion from Troy, he found only about twenty giants remaining, of which Gogmagog was the biggest and strongest.

It is said that Gogmagog was twelve feet tall and so strong that he could tear up an oak tree as if it were a hazel wand. From Geoffrey of Monmouth, we learn of what occurred next.

Brutus arrived at Totnes in Devon and renamed the islands 'Britain' after himself. With Brutus came Corineus, a courageous warrior and champion, who became the founder of 'Cornwall'. It was said that Corineus loved nothing better than being able to fight a giant and that he could 'overthrow him as easily as if he were fighting against a mere boy'.

One day, Brutus and his men were enjoying a festival in Totnes when Gogmagog and twenty other giants attacked and killed many of the Britons. The Britons fought back and, with the help of Corineus, slew them all except for Gogmagog. Brutus ordered that his life be spared because he wanted Corineus to publicly wrestle with him.

Corineus was pleased to be given this opportunity to fight Gogmagog and took off his armour. The contest began and each approached and wrapped his arms around the other. Gogmagog broke three of his opponent's ribs, angering him to such an extent that he charged at the giant and, summoning all of his strength, heaved him on to his shoulders and ran with him to the nearby coast.

Corineus then climbed to the top of a mighty cliff and hurled the monster over the side, where he fell on the sharp rocks of the reef and was dashed to pieces. This place is still called Gogmagog's Leap.

Another story says that Gogmagog, instead of being killed, was carried in chains to London, a new city built by Brutus and at that time called Troya Nova, or New Troy. The giant, until the end of his life, was given the job of guarding the city from attack.

By Tudor times the story had become very widespread and the giants had achieved status as the protectors of London. In 1554 when Philip of Spain and Queen Mary arrived in London they were met at the drawbridge on London Bridge by 'two greate giants … one nemed Corineus Brittanus … the other Gogmagog Albionus'. The giants also became enshrined in the London Guildhall and a regular feature of the Mayor's Parade.

Within two decades the name Gogmagog was used to refer to the hills near Cambridge, possibly because of the existence of the image of a giant carved on one of them. A number of accounts from the early seventeenth to the mid-eighteenth century refer to this image and in 1640 John Layer noted: 'I could never learn how these hills came to be called Gog Magog Hills, unless it were from a high and mighty portraiture of a giant which the Schollars of Cambridge cut upon the turf …'

Even in relatively recent times, to the north of the hills, children in the village of Cherry Hinton were not allowed to play in a nearby chalk pit as it was said that the giants Gog and Magog were buried there, and if they were woken 'they may come after you'. This

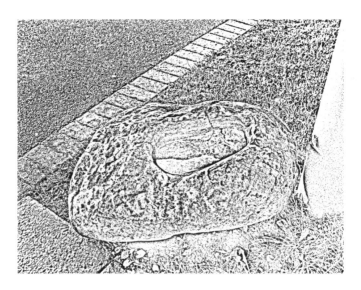

belief was explored in *Notes & Queries* (1874) by H.C. Lofts, who heard the tale form an elderly man living in the neighbourhood:

> It asserts that previous to the formation of these hills (Which are three in number), and near to the same spot, was a very large cave, which was inhabited by a giant and his wife (a giantess) of extraordinary stature, whose names were Gog and Magog. They did not live very happily together, for scarcely a day passed by without a quarrel between them. On one occasion the giantess so outraged the giant, that he swore he would destroy her life. She instantly fled from the cave; he quickly pursued her; but she running faster than her husband, he could not overtake her. Gog, in his anger, stooped down, took up a handful of earth and threw at her; it missed her, but where it fell it raised a hill, which is seen to the present day. Again the enraged giant threw earth at his wife, but again it missed her; where it fell it was the cause of the second hill. Magog still kept up her pace; but again the giant, in his rage, threw more earth at his wife; but this time it completely buried her alive, and where she fell is marked by the highest hill of the three. So runs, the local tradition respecting the origin of the Gog-Magog Hills.

On the outskirts of Cherry Hinton, on the junction of Fulbourn Road and the High Street, there is a place known locally as the Giant's Grave. Also called Springhead Pool, The Spring or Robin Hood Dip, a signboard at this public park, states that '… the origins of the name may be the giant Magog, but the name may also have come from some unusually tall skeletons in Iron Age burials which were unearthed locally on Lime Kiln Hill'.

Over the road from the Giant's Grave, in the car park of The Robin Hood pub, there survives a dark sarsen stone. This lonely megalith is about three feet across with a large, but recognisably human-shaped 'size 10 footprint' seemingly carved out of it.

PC PEAK OF WICKEN FEN

On a Friday evening in August 1855 a young man set off under
the waxing moon from his home in Burwell to his job as the village
policeman for Wicken. The 24-year-old Police Constable Peak kissed
his pregnant wife goodbye, and his 1-year-old son, and went off to
attend the hay auction at The Red Lion public house on Pond Green.

PC26 Richard Peak had joined the Cambridgeshire
Constabulary just before Christmas almost three years earlier.
At five feet and ten inches tall, he was described as a 'steady and
respectable man'.

On that August evening, as was customary for such duty, Peak
was not wearing his day uniform, but was dressed in a pair of
coarse uniform trousers, a dark cloth vest, a black neck tie, a check
coat and a brown great coat, along with a pair of wellington boots.

The sale had finished by 9 p.m., but forty or fifty people
remained drinking on the premises, and so Peak continued to pay
periodic visits to the pub, whilst 'pounding the beat'. By about
3.15 a.m. the premises were empty, and the only noticeable incident during the evening had been when Peak had removed two
troublemakers at the request of the landlord.

On leaving the pub, Peak said to the landlord, 'Good morning,
I've got an hour and a half's walk, then I will go to bed.' The
journey from the pub should have taken him across the fen to
North Street, Burwell, where he was due to have a brief meeting
with an officer from an adjoining beat at 4 a.m. before the end of
his shift.

However, Peak never made the meeting and was never seen
again. There were no signs of the clothes he wore or the staff and
handcuffs that he carried. Did he ever follow the Maltings footpath,
or make it across the footbridge over Monks' Lode and along the
well-trodden path skirting the peat bogs and cornfields to Burwell?

When Peak had failed to return for duty on Monday morning, a
search of the area was ordered and 'not a drop of water that would
float a cork within three miles' was left uninspected. A notification

was also sent to all the ports and police stations in the kingdom, requesting everyone to be on the lookout for information about Peak.

The investigation showed that, during the whole of the fateful evening, Peak had consumed just one shilling's worth of brandy and water, along with a pint of beer, and by the early hours of the morning the landlord regarded him as sober. Witnesses also recalled that, at four o'clock in the morning, three drunken men had been seen fighting in the streets of Wicken, but Peak was not among them.

The fate of PC Peak has, since that time, been the subject of much speculation. Some say he absconded, others that he was murdered and his body buried in the peat bogs.

It was also said that a local man once made a deathbed confession that, 'Peak had been hit on the head and burnt in a ... brick kiln.' The dying man said he knew who did it but gave no name, and despite one informant saying that a strange smell had emanated from the kiln following the disappearance, investigations at the kiln on the village side of Wicken Sedge Fen, half a mile from Peak's route, proved fruitless. It was even rumoured that crown buttons had been raked from ashes in the kiln, but Peak had not been wearing his uniform that night.

The police historians Ken Watson and Chief Supt Les Waters, having studied the case in great depth, have been unable to find any reason for Peak having enemies in the area, or any motive for his being killed.

An online site with tributes to serving police officers who have died in the line of duty records the following:

Richard Peak
Police Constable
Cambridgeshire Constabulary
Died 18 August 1855, aged 24

Went missing from his beat at Wicken in the early hours in suspicious circumstances, he had earlier been involved in a disturbance and it was suspected he was murdered by a local gang but his body was never found.

The same site also includes the following entry for another Cambridgeshire man:

Thomas Saunders Lamb
Constable
Borough of Huntingdon
Died 23 December 1841, aged 28
Found drowned in the River Ouse some weeks after going missing from his beat in suspicious circumstances in the early hours, when it is believed he was assaulted by several persons and thrown off a bridge into the river.

In 2007 I had the pleasure of hearing the late Arthur Dunham of March tell the story of George the Stockman, which had undoubtedly been influenced by the above accounts.

George was an old man, and set in his ways. Every night he would walk a mile or two from his home out on Binnimoor Fen to the local pub, where he would always sit in the same seat and always drink the same pint from the same jug.

One night when George got to the pub he found another man sitting in his favourite seat. He was furious and asked the man to move, but the interloper would not budge. The two men got into an argument and George stormed off home, muttering that he 'would never go to that pub again ...' and 'I'll get him for it later ...'

Well, the next morning, the other man was found badly beaten down by the river and the new constable from March police station was sent on his bicycle out on to the fen to arrest George. But, whilst all the local people showed great respect for the policeman, none of them seemed able to help him find George's house.

It was not until the following afternoon that the duty sergeant realised that the young policeman had not returned to the station, or to his home for that matter. A search party was sent out and in time his bicycle was found – half in, half out of the Old River Nene, the back wheel spinning in the breeze, but the young man's body was never found.

About a week after the incident in the pub, George the Stockman was seen shovelling the stack. It was also noted by the neighbours that the cattle were giving the stack a wide berth, and that a strange smell was coming from that direction. When asked, George said it was dead foxes that had burrowed their way in amongst the straw.

The information was passed to the police, and once again George received a visit from a constable, this time one who knew where he lived. He questioned the old man for some time and went away satisfied that he had not seen the young police constable.

But not too many years later, after old George had died and they were clearing out his cottage, the local people found three police buttons in his old button pot!

James Wentworth Day also related a version of the story of PC Peak in his *A History of the Fens* (and repeated it in *Rum owd Boys*), though he misquotes the name.

In this account, which he heard from his uncle's one-time bailiff, Bob King, he describes how Peacock 'was killed after he tried to stop a Saturday night brawl in the Maid's Head Inn'.

Day states that Jim Bacon and another 'Fen Tiger' had followed the constable outside and bludgeoned the constable to death. They then hid his body in a turf barrow before wheeling it over the Breddes to the brick kiln for cremation. The truncheon, according to Day, was dredged up many years later from one of the pits.

Such was the personal quality of Bob King's storytelling that he also alleged that he had been driving his master's horse and trap to Upware on the morning after the supposed murder, when Jim Bacon and the other man suddenly appeared out of the hedge on their way to the ferry. Bob then noticed that the men had blood-stained hands and remarked on this.

'We bin a-pig-killin'!' Jim Bacon is said to have replied, as they carried on their way. According to Bob, the men were never seen again.

Day also recalled a family story of the deathbed confession of a woman in the almshouses, who he said called for his mother and gave her an old letter with an American postmark. The dying woman said that she had kept the letter, which was from her son, for thirty years or more but could not read, and so did not know what the letter contained. She wished to hear the contents before she died.

The letter, said Day, 'told the lady that the two murderers, one of whom was her son, had got safely to Liverpool, taken ship to America, and were working and prospering'.

As noted above, research on the deathbed confession has proven it to be unfounded. But, as Gillian Peak (Richard Peak's great-granddaughter, who has carried out her own research on the mystery) likes to say, with regards to these accounts of her grandfather's disappearance ... James Wentworth Day 'never let the truth get in the way of a good story'.

THE FRENCH PRISONERS AT NORMAN CROSS

Just beside the A15 London Road, and not far from the junction with the A1M at Norman Cross, there can be seen a pillar topped by a bronze eagle. This sculpture was unveiled in 2005, by the Duke of Wellington, to replace an earlier memorial to the 1,800 prisoners who died at the first purpose-built camp that held those captured during the Napoleonic Wars.

The previous memorial, which had been unveiled in 1914, had been vandalised in 1990 and the eagle stolen. An appeal had raised the money to restore the memorial, but it also needed to be moved from its site by the side of the old A1 to its new situation as the major road was being upgraded to the A1M.

The camp, or depot, as it was then known, though contemporary accounts also call it the Stilton or Yaxley Barracks, is a source of a number of interesting stories, some of which I would like to tell you, but first it would be good to say a few words about the history of the place.

During the revolutionary and Napoleonic Wars of 1793–1815, a huge number of prisoners were taken in sea and land battles. Initially old forts and prison hulks were used for containing these prisoners of war, but these were proving inadequate.

The site was chosen as it was close to the Great North Road and not far from the Fenland waterways, which enabled easy transportation from the coast. The other benefit of the site was that it was quite far inland, making escape and rescue attempts challenging. It was also seen as somewhere that could supply sufficient fresh food for the predicted large influx of prisoners.

The first prisoners arrived at the camp in March 1797 and, at its peak, it held over 7,000 mainly French sailors and soldiers. Compared to France, Norman Cross was much colder, and with the French government refusing to pay for either the prisoners' food or clothing, many of the men were extremely uncomfortable.

Eventually the British government provided uniforms for the prisoners, made with yellow cloth and with red waistcoats to enable them to be easily seen and recognised. But with so many men in such a confined space there was much disease. It has been calculated that more than 1,000 prisoners died during a typhoid epidemic in 1800 and 1801, and another 800 prisoners died during the two decades of the prison's existence.

The prisoners often arrived in England via the port at King's Lynn. Accounts describe how: 'At Lynn the prisoners were packed into barges and lighters and were sent up river through the Forty Foot, the Hundred Foot, the Pauper's Cut, and the Nene to Peterborough whence they marched to Norman Cross.'

The novelist George Borrow recalled making the journey as a child with his mother, across the Fens from King's Lynn to Peterborough when the Wash and the Fenlands were flooded. They were en route to visit his father who was stationed at Norman Cross:

> The country was ... submerged entirely drowned no land was visible; the trees were growing bolt upright in the flood, whilst farmhouses and cottages were standing insulated; the horses which drew us were up to the knees in water, and, on coming to blind pools and 'greedy depths,' were not in-frequently swimming, in which case the boys or urchins who mounted them sometimes stood, sometimes knelt, upon the saddle and pillions. No accident, however, occurred either to the quadrupeds or bipeds, who appeared respectively to be quite au fait in their business, and extricated themselves with the greatest ease from places in which Pharaoh and all his host would have gone to the bottom. Nightfall brought us to Peterborough, and from thence we were not slow in reaching the place of our destination.

This complex journey also enabled escape attempts to become commonplace, and the accounts describe how one prisoner was shot dead trying to escape by jumping into the water at Peterborough; another, who was quartered overnight in the city, was shot trying to run from the lodgings.

Three other men escaped on the journey to the depot in April 1797 and the following month: 'Early on Tuesday 800 or 900 French prisoners went through Wisbech from Lynn bound for Yaxley. The French Captain escaped from the Purfleet.'

The manager in charge of the prison traffic between the coast and Norman Cross recorded how, though the majority of the prisoners were eventually recaptured, they had shown much ingenuity in their attempts to deceive the prison guards, including the use of counterfeit money as bribes.

Prisoners who did not manage to escape on the journey to Norman Cross often attempted to do so when they reached their destination. In June 1797 two French prisoners escaped but were retaken at Wisbech, and were conveyed back to the prison 'to more solitary and secure quarters'.

In December of the same year an officer succeeded in escaping and, in April 1801, some prisoners escaped, though three were recaptured at Boston. Of this group, three others stole a fishing boat and succeeded in getting out to sea, only to be recaptured on the Norfolk coast by a custom house cutter.

Saunders recorded how in July 1804, when the depot was very crowded:

> prisoners cut down a part of the wood enclosure during the night, and nine of them escaped. In another part of the prison, as soon as daylight broke, it was discovered they had undermined a distance of 34 feet towards the Great North Road, under the Fosse which surrounded the prison, although it was four feet deep, and it was not discovered that they had any tools. They had not, however, carried the mine a sufficient extent for it to answer their purpose. Five of them who escaped were re-taken in the course of a few days, but the others got clear away.

In August 1813, five French prisoners who had escaped from Norman Cross were retaken by some farmer's servants in Hampshire while on their way to the coast in order to get to France.

Did Chafer Legge's ancestor play a part in helping the escape of some of the Norman Cross prisoners? The tale 'French Prisoners in the Fens' alleges that he did: I have adapted below the tale that was printed in *Tales from the Fens*.

The Fenman, Grey Goose Feathers and the French Prisoners of War

One day, whilst visiting Ely Fair, young Noah saw a pretty girl surrounded by a gang of ruffians. He soon gathered that they were trying to steal her purse and so he rushed forward to help her. Little did he realise but this action would change his life and make him a part of history.

The gang turned on Noah, allowing the girl to escape, but she soon came back with assistance in the form of the travelling showmen. The gang was soon dispersed and Noah was carried into one of the caravans so that his wounds could be nursed and, to his delight, the pretty girl was helping with this!

Noah and the girl soon became firm friends, and he also became her escort in touring the Fens. She paid for him to stay at The Ship Inn at Brandon Creek, and from there they would travel out in a pony and cart each day to explore the area, which he knew very well from years spent fishing and fowling with his father.

In time the girl, who seemed to have a ready supply of money, purchased a sailing boat with two cabins, and Noah sailed her around the further reaches of the flatland until one day they came across a small farmhouse by the Little Ouse, close to Shrub Hill on Hockwold Fen, and at least three miles from the nearest neighbours.

The girl thought the place was perfect and asked the couple who lived there if she could lodge with them. At first they were reluctant, but the offer she made to them would more than pay for her bed and board, and so they took her in. She soon became almost like a daughter to them.

Noah, however, continued to sleep on the boat, and one day the girl asked him to take her over to Peterborough. They went by

Salter's Lode to Wisbech and then down the Nene. The journey took about two weeks and, during this time, Noah noticed that the girl never wasted an opportunity to talk to bargemen on the way.

On reaching Peterborough, Noah moored the boat and the girl went off on her own. She returned three days later greatly upset but, despite coaxing, she would not tell Noah what had occurred. She merely reassured him that she was fine.

They sailed back to Shrub Hill and carried on as before, with the girl staying in the farmhouse and Noah living in the cabin and continuing his usual profession.

One night, Noah was woken by the sound of a barge drawing up alongside his. He climbed out of his bunk and went out to see what was happening, only to see the girl hugging two men, and then kissing one of them. She then took the two men into the farmhouse with her.

The next morning, as soon as he got the chance, Noah asked the girl who the two men were, only to be told that one was her brother, and the other her fiancée. He asked what they were doing there, and she made Noah swear on the little silver cross that she wore around her neck that he would not tell a soul what she was about to tell him.

Noah agreed to this and she told him how the two men had been prisoners of war at the Norman Cross depot but that the French government would not pay their ransoms or even send enough to provided basic care for them. She also explained how she had not only been getting help from the travelling showmen, but also from the farmer and his wife, the latter of which had fetched a goose quill for her and cut it down the middle. He had thereby made her a member of the Brotherhood of the Grey Goose Feather and from then on she was guaranteed the help of any other Fenmen who were members of the Brotherhood (which reappears later in this book, during a Civil War tale).

And so Noah was taken into the farmhouse to see the two men, and also became a member of the brotherhood. He was appalled at how thin and gaunt the Frenchmen looked, and when two more arrived in the same condition he decided to travel to Norman Cross to see for himself what was happening.

Noah gathered a load of grey goose feathers, which he carefully split down the middle, and got himself a job driving the towing horse of a barge that was travelling to Stanground. When they reached their destination, Noah walked to Norman Cross and soon gained a position as cook for the soldiers. It was not long before the prisoners got to know that if they were able to escape and they took half a feather with them, they could get help across the Fens to Shrub Hill and to safety.

One day a Frenchman with a feather arrived at Shrub Hill to say that the Englishman who had given it to him had been put in the gaol for fighting with the officers. The girl and the farmer immediately set off towards Peterborough, but by the time they got to Wisbech they met Noah coming the other way. He had shown his feather to the gaoler and found the door of his cell unlocked the next morning!

Their way back home took them to King's Lynn where they chatted to some fishermen and some of the sailors from the ships bringing French wine into the town. They found that the ships often returned empty and so a deal was made that would prove useful later.

When they reached Shrub Hill they discovered that some soldiers had been asking in the area if anyone had seen any 'froggies' as a lot had escaped from Norman Cross! Noah replied that there was no place for frogs there, as it was smothered with snakes and vipers!

The soldiers went on their way but Noah immediately built a shelter out at the 'duck decoy' in a quiet spot, where the Frenchmen could hide during the day. Eventually a fishing boat from King's Lynn arrived and a dozen prisoners were loaded onto it and taken, with Noah and the girl, up to Denver, then King's Lynn, and out to sea where they met up with a ship at anchor.

Sometime later, after even more Frenchmen had been enabled to escape, the young woman's brother and lover arrived, accompanied by a priest. The couple were married and they set off back to

France, leaving Noah as the owner of a two-cabin boat and with lots of tales to tell to his grandson!

Of the prisoners who did not manage, or attempt, to escape from the depot, most kept themselves occupied by attending classes in languages, mathematics, dancing and navigation. Open-air kitchens were provided in which prisoners prepared their own food using local produce and their meat rations.

The leftover bones from animals and fish were carved into intricate models, particularly ships, mechanical toys and domino sets. Straw was also obtained and woven into objects such as cigar cases, jewellery boxes, calling card holders and pictures. Many of the objects were sold at the regular market outside the prison gates, with model sailing ships selling for as much as £40. The money from the sales was retained by the prisoners.

The prisoners also engaged in more nefarious activities, such as the printing of counterfeit money, and making obscene pictures and carvings. The latter trade became so common that the respectable inhabitants of Peterborough complained to the authorities.

On 18 December 1808 the market was closed with the threat that it would not be opened until 'those that make and sell the toys and drawings' were named. This was viewed as a very severe punishment, as it also stopped the supply of vegetables, condiments, tobacco, sugar, beer and clothes, which were viewed as 'little necessaries, luxuries, and comforts' by the prisoners. It also stopped them from selling their legitimate manufactures. Eventually the men who were controlling the illicit traffic were found and sent to the prison hulks at Chatham.

Peace between England and France was finally declared in 1814. Saunders described the scene:

> the joy amongst the prisoners was of an extravagant description. A
> large white flag was set up in each of the quadrangles of the Depot,

under which the thousands of poor fellows who had been for years in confinement … danced, sung, laughed, and cried for joy … The prisoners were so elated at the prospect of being liberated that they ceased to perform any work. They were all bent on selling their stock, which they did at 50 per cent, advanced price. Many of them had realized fortunes of from £500 to £1000 each in Bank of England notes.

By June, all the prisoners had left, and the following September the ammunition stored there was removed. Two years afterwards – in June 1816 – the building was pulled down and the materials sold by auction.

Now all that is left to show of this once important site is the memorial and the names on the map. The site where 7,000 men were once held captive is now a pasture field. However, a superb collection of about 800 items made by the prisoners at Norman Cross can be seen at the Peterborough City Museum and Art Gallery, where there is a dedicated gallery for such exhibits. More of such items can also be seen at the King's Lynn Museum.

THE SUFFERINGS OF ELIZABETH WOODCOCK

She was in prison, as you see,
All in a cave of snow;
And she could not relieved be,
Though she was frozen so.
Ah, well-a-day!
For she was all froze in with frost,
Eight days and nights, poor soul;
But when they gave her up for lost,
They found her down the hole,
Ah, well-a-day!

The above rhyme is from a manuscript ballad included in Hone's *Every-Day Book*, volume 2 (1838). The book includes an account of the true experience of a Cambridgeshire woman at the very end of the eighteenth century. This event became the stuff of a number of folk tales and, as such, appears in various collections. I thought that it would be good to go back to an early source of the story and relate it in as accurate a way as possible:

Elizabeth Woodcock, aged 42 years, went on horseback from Impington to Cambridge, on Saturday, being market day, 2 February 1799. On her return home in the evening, between six and seven o'clock, being about half a mile from her own house, her horse started at a sudden light, which proceeded, most probably, from a meteor … She was herself struck with the light, and exclaimed, 'Good God! what can this be!'

It was a very inclement stormy night, a bleak wind blew from the north-east. The ground was covered by great quantities of snow that had fallen during the day, yet it was not spread uniformly over the surface. The deepest ditches were completely filled up, whilst on the open fields there was but a thin covering; but in many parts it had accumulated to a considerable depth, nowhere yet so as to render the way impassable, but still enough to retard and impede the traveller.

The horse, upon his starting, ran backwards and approached the brink of a ditch; the poor woman, fearing lest the animal should plunge into it, dismounted. Her intention was to walk and to lead the horse home; but he started again, and broke from her. She repeated her attempt to take hold of the bridle, but the horse turned suddenly out of the road and directed his steps over the common field.

Elizabeth followed the horse, but she lost one of her shoes in the snow. Already wearied with the exertion, and with a heavy basket on her arm ... her pursuit of the horse was greatly impeded; she persisted, however, and followed him through an opening in a hedge, a little beyond which she overtook him (about a quarter of a mile from the place where she alighted) and, taking hold of the bridle, made another attempt to lead him home.

But she found herself so much fatigued and exhausted, her hands and feet numb with cold – particularly her left foot, which was without a shoe – that she was unable to proceed further. Sitting down then upon the ground in this state, and letting go the bridle, 'Tinker,' she said, calling the horse by his name, 'I am too much tired to go any farther, you must go home without me,' and exclaimed, 'Lord have mercy upon me! What will become of me!'

The ground on which she sat was level with the field, under the thicket. There was then but a small quantity of snow near her, but it accumulated so rapidly that when Chesterton bell rang at eight o'clock she was completely enclosed by it. The depth of the snow in which she was enveloped was about six feet in a perpendicular direction and two or three feet over her head. Her imprisonment was now complete, for she was incapable of making any effectual attempt to extricate herself and, in addition to her fatigue and cold, her clothes were stiffened by the frost.

Resigning herself calmly to her bad situation, she sat awaiting the dawn. To the best of her recollection she slept very little during the first night (or, indeed, any of the succeeding nights or days, except six days later on Friday 8 February). Early the next morning she heard the ringing of a bell at one of the villages a small distance away. Her mind was now turned to thoughts of her preservation, and to ensuring that anyone who chanced to come near the place might discover her.

On the first morning after her imprisonment, observing a circular hole in the snow, about two feet in length and half a foot in diameter, she broke off a branch from a bush that was close to her, and with it thrust her handkerchief through the hole, and hung it as a signal of distress upon one of the uppermost twigs that remained uncovered.

She perfectly distinguished the alterations of day and night, and heard the bells of her own and some of the neighbouring villages. She was also sensible of the living scene around her, frequently noticing the sound of carriages upon the road, the natural cries of animals, such as the bleating of sheep and lambs, and the barking of dogs. She frequently shouted out, but the snow prevented the transmission of her voice, so that no one heard her.

One day, finding her left hand beginning to swell, she took two rings – the tokens of her nuptial vows – from her finger and put them, together with a little money that she had in her pocket, into a small box, sensibly judging that, should she not be found alive, the rings and money were less likely to be overlooked by the discoverers of her breathless corpse.

When the period of her seclusion approached its termination, and a thaw took place on the Friday after the commencement of her misfortunes, she felt uncommonly faint and languid; her clothes were wet quite through by the melted snow; the aperture before-mentioned became considerably enlarged, and tempted her to make an effort to release herself.

Alas! It was a vain attempt; her strength was too much impaired; her feet and legs were no longer obedient to her will, and her clothes were heavier by the water that they had imbibed. For the first time, she began to despair of ever being discovered or taken out alive. She sat with one of her hands spread over her face, and fetched the deepest sighs; her breath was short and difficult, and symptoms of approaching dissolution became every hour more alarming.

On Sunday, 10 February, a young farmer, whose name is Muncey, on his way home from Cambridge at about 12.30 p.m., crossed the open field and passed very near the spot where the woman was stuck in the snow. The coloured handkerchief hanging upon the tops of the twigs caught his eye; he walked up to the place and, seeing an opening in the snow, he looked in and saw a female figure, whom he recognised to be the woman who had been so long missing. He didn't speak to her but, seeing another young farmer and the shepherd at a little distance, he communicated to them the discovery he had made, and though they scarcely gave any credit to his report, they went with him to the spot.

The shepherd called out, 'Are you there, Elizabeth Woodcock?'

She replied, in a faint and feeble accent, 'Dear John Stittle, I know your voice; for God's sake help me out of this place!'

Stittle made his way through the snow till he was able to reach her; she eagerly grasped his hand, and implored him not to leave her. 'I have been here a long time,' she observed.

'Yes,' answered the man, 'ever since Saturday.'

'Aye, Saturday week,' she replied. 'I have heard the bells go two Sundays for church.'

Mr Muncey and Mr Merrington Jr went to the village to inform Elizabeth's husband, and to procure proper means for conveying her home. They quickly returned with her husband, some of the neighbours, and the elder Mr Merrington, who brought with him his horse and chaise-cart, blankets to wrap her in, and some refreshment, which he took it for granted she would be in peculiar need of partaking.

The snow being slightly cleared away, Mr Merrington went up to her and gave her a piece of biscuit and a small quantity of brandy. As he took her up to put her into the chaise, the stocking of her left leg, adhering to the ground, came off. She fainted in his arms, being very much exhausted; and the motion, added to the impression that the sight of her husband and neighbours made upon her, was too much for her strength and spirits. When she recovered, her husband laid her gently in the carriage, covered her with the blankets and conveyed her without delay or interruption to her own house.

Mr Okes, a surgeon, first saw her in the cart. She spoke to him with a voice tolerably strong, but rather hoarse: her hands and arms were sodden, but not very cold, though her legs and feet were. She was immediately put to bed, and weak broth given to her occasionally.

Elizabeth's husband later explained that when the horse had come home, he and another person had set out on the road with a lantern, and went to Cambridge, where they had learnt that she left the inn at six o'clock that evening. They had explored the road that night, and for four succeeding days, and began to fear that she had been robbed and murdered.

From the time of her being lost she had eaten only snow, and believed she had not slept till Friday 8 February; her only evacuation was a little water. The hurry of spirits, occasioned by too many visitors, rendered her feverish; and her feet were found to be completely mortified from being frostbitten before she was covered with snow.

She was so disturbed by company that Mr Okes had little hope of her recovery. He ordered a mutton broth enema, a saline mixture, medicinal wine, a strong decoction of bark and three grains of opium in the course of a day. He opened the blisters on her feet and continued the use of brandy, enemas, opium, bark and port wine.

By 17 April the sores were free from dead skin and daily lessened; her appetite was tolerably good and her general health began to mend; but with all these circumstances in her favour, she felt herself to be very uncomfortable and, in fact, her prospect was most miserable. For though her life was saved, the mutilated state in which she was left, without even a chance of being ever able to attend to the duties of her family, was almost worse than death itself. The loss, too, of all her toes must have made it impossible for her to move herself but with the assistance of crutches.

Mr Okes ascribed the preservation of her life to her not having slept or had any evacuations under the snow, and to her resignation and the calm state of her mind.

The two-part 'Account of the providential preservation of Elizabeth Woodcock, who survived a confinement under the snow of nearly eight days and nights in the month of February, 1799', was written by the minister of the parish and the surgeon, for her benefit, and went through two editions. Prints from drawings of her in the snow and in her bed were also sold.

Sadly, Elizabeth's lingering existence came to an end on 13 July 1799. On the burial notice the following note was written: 'She was in a state of intoxication when she was lost. Her death was accelerated (to say the least) by spirituous liquors afterwards taken, procured by the donations of various visitors.'

The story of what happened to Elizabeth spread around the country, and numerous engravings of her were published at the time. Over the years, the facts of the case have been altered and, in at least one account, the story even moved to just before Christmas. In this account Elizabeth was carrying a basket of Christmas provisions, which she ate, including the tallow candles when the food ran out. This story also expanded the time of her captivity to seven weeks rather than seven days, and her death was alleged to have happened on the way home. It is also said that on her way home Elizabeth had stopped for a glass of gin (by no means the first of that day) at The Three Tuns (a seventeenth-century inn demolished in 1936) in Castle Street.

In the Cambridge Museum (formerly the Folk Museum) there are a set of nutcrackers that are said to have been purchased by Elizabeth Woodcock at Cambridge Market on that fateful day, along with some nuts. It is said that she ate them to keep up her strength whilst hidden under the snow.

Another account describes how Mr Muncey, who discovered Elizabeth's whereabouts, had dreamed that if he visited a particular spot he would find a trapped hare. When he awoke he could still see the agonised look in the hare's eyes and so he went to the site and saw a red handkerchief tied to a twig. He then found the woman.

Mr Muncey later became parish clerk for Impington, a post he held for fifty years. Perhaps it was at his instigation that a memorial was placed at the site where Elizabeth had been trapped. The memorial was replaced fifty years later and the original stone also donated to the Cambridge Museum. There is still a stone to mark the episode, in one of the fields on Chiver's farm. This monument, which is about eight feet high, can be seen when travelling on the guided busway.

The monument consists of a round pillar standing on a cube about three feet each way. The wording on the cube, which is very worn and impossible to read in places, is as follows:

IN MEMORY OF/ ELIZ. WOODCOCK./
LOST ON THIS SPOT IN A SNOW/STORM WHILE RETURNING/
FROM CAMBRIDGE MARKET/ FEB 2 1799/
SHE WAS DISCOVERED/ EIGHT DAYS AFTER. 7 FEET/
BENEATH THE SNOW ALIVE &/IN POSSESSION OF ALL HER/
SENSES/AND DIED JULY 24 OF THE SAME YEAR. AGED 42 …
M WOODCOCK WAS FOUND BY WM. MUNCEY. THE PRESENT CHURCH CLERK/
AT IMPINGTON./ THE ORIGINAL STONE RECORDING/
THIS EVENT BEING MUCH DEFACED/AFTER/

STANDING 50 YEARS/THIS MONUMENT WAS ERECTED/
BY SUBSCRIPTION. JUNE 19.1849.

The cottage where Elizabeth lived, and where she was visited by many people, survives at Station Road, Impington, near to the war memorial, and on the wall can be seen a commemorative plaque.

6

OF CHURCHES, PARSONS AND SAINTS

This chapter commences with a tale that was constructed from a storytelling performance on St Etheldreda (or Æthelthryth as she should correctly be known) that I gave in Wimblington church in 2005. It is based on extensive research using many historical and folk tale sources. This is followed by the apparently true story of Bricstan of Chatteris, a twelfth-century novice monk who received divine protection from Etheldreda. The third part of the chapter comprises a number of tales from around the county about the siting of churches. The chapter ends with the original accounts of the stories told about Whirlin' (or Whirlwind) Sunday, and the origin of the practice in the Wisbech area. It has been speculated that the Wisbech Lenten festivities are actually a corruption of Careling (or Carlin') Sunday, found in other counties. Before we commence, I would like to relate a short rhyme that illustrates the significance and generosity of the local abbeys in medieval times:

Ramsey, rich in gold and fee
Thorney, flower of many fine tree,
Crowland, the courteous of meat and drink
Spalding, the gluttons as all men do think,
Peterborough the proud, as all men do say,
Sawtry, by the way, that old Abbay
Gave more alms in one day, than all of they!

ETHELDREDA – PRINCESS, ABBESS AND SAINT

Etheldreda was born in Exning, Suffolk *c.* AD 636, at a time of great change, when many important people were converting from paganism to Christianity. The people had been worshipping the old gods including Tiwaz, Woden, Thor and Frig, whose names we remember in the days of the week – Tuesday, Wednesday, Thursday and Friday. Now they would worship just one God.

At that time Christian Irish monks were spreading the word down from the north, from St Columba who founded the monastery on Iona. Meanwhile, the Roman Church, brought to England by St Augustine on a mission from Pope Gregory, was spreading the word from the south.

Etheldreda was brought up in a Christian household. One of the daughters of Anna, nephew of Raedwald, the High King of the East Angles, her father had been baptised in Kent by Augustine, and became king himself, when she was just 10 years old.

The royal family probably moved to the Palace of Rendlesham on the coast of the lands of the South Folk (Suffolk). The church there was called St Gregory's and the Great Hall was the place where, it is said, the epic poem *Beowulf* was performed. The poem ends in the description of the death and burial of the hero king:

> Then the Geats built a barrow on the headland – it was high and broad, visible from far to all seafarers; in ten days they built the beacon for that courageous man; and they constructed as noble an enclosure as wise men could devise, to enshrine the ashes.
>
> They buried rings and brooches in the barrow, all those adornments that brave men had brought out from the hoard after Beowulf died. They bequeathed the gleaming gold, treasure of men, to the earth, and there it still remains as useless to men as it was before.

Living in the Palace at Rendlesham, Etheldreda would have grown up with the tales of Raedwald and would have seen his burial

mound, across the water at what we now know as Sutton Hoo, the place that was very like that described in the *Beowulf* poem.

Raedwald had died just six years before Etheldreda was born. Bede tells us that in his temple at Rendlesham he set up a Christian altar alongside a pagan one! For him, it seems, Christianity meant the acceptance of an additional god, not the abandonment of his ancestral heathen ones!

When Etheldreda was 17, Hilda, a devout nun from Northumbria, who had trained under the Irish monk who had founded Lindisfarne, stayed at the court. She would later prove to be influential in Etheldreda's life.

Hilda knew Bishop Felix who led a monastic school at Dunwich, which after his death was run by Thomas of the Girvii, and it was probably this connection that led to the marriage of Etheldreda with Tonbert of the South Girvii of the Fenland area. He died shortly after the marriage and Etheldreda gained control of the Isle of Ely.

Etheldreda's father and her brother were killed fighting against the pagan Penda of Mercia in 654 and, the following, year Penda was in turn killed by Oswy, the king of the Northumbrians. Oswy was a Celtic Christian and his wife was Roman Christian. Both were instrumental, along with Hilda and Bishop Wilfred of York, in the Council of Whitby, at which the date of Easter was set.

When Etheldreda was 29 she was betrothed by her uncle Ethelwald, the new king of the East Angles, to marry Egfrid, the young son of King Oswy who was twelve years younger than her. She was sent to live in his household. Egfrid was probably not the easiest of men to get along with; as well as being so much younger than his wife, he had experienced a difficult childhood. He was held hostage for a number of years in the court of King Penda of Mercia and it was only when Penda died that he was freed to go home.

On her journey north, Etheldreda would have seen a number of monasteries including Hilda's new abbey at Whitby. She may have seen Lindisfarne and the Irish Celtic monasteries, built in the Celtic model with small wattle and daub with thatch houses nestled closely together surrounded by a bank and ditch.

Etheldreda soon came under the influence of Wilfred of York, and decided that she wanted to become a nun and consequently not to consummate her new marriage.

In 670 Egfrid, on the death of his father, became king. However, despite much persuasion, his wife of some ten years, and yet still a virgin, still wanted to become a nun. In despair he granted her permission to take the veil at the Irish-influenced monastery of Coldingham, near Berwick, under St Ebba, his aunt.

She set off for Coldingham and was given her veil and habit by Bishop Wilfred. But her new life was short-lived as Egfrid changed his mind and wanted her to be his wife again. He set off to find her and bring her back to resume her marital role.

On hearing that Egfrid was on his way, Etheldreda left Coldingham and headed south, planning to return to the Isle of Ely. During the journey she stopped for a rest at the top of a hill at West Halton by the River Humber. Whilst she and her attendants rested, the sea left its natural channel to surround the hill. The women stayed there for seven days, praying.

Egfrid saw what had happened and, unable to reach his wife, he gave up and returned to York. Etheldreda went back to Ely to found a double monastery. On the way she stopped again for a rest at a spot 'sprinkled with flowers of many colours, and fresh with sweet scented roses'. There she put her staff in the ground and fell asleep, and when she woke it had rooted and turned into an ash tree with branches covered with green bark and leaves.

Etheldreda's monastery was built on the lands she received from her first marriage. At that time it was still a very desolate place in the midst of the Fens. On the other side of this flat expanse, at Crowland, Guthlac described creatures he saw in the marsh as a hermit – wicked sprites, with filthy beards, shaggy ears, horses teeth, scabby thighs, knotty knees, crooked legs and splayed feet.

Not surprisingly, Etheldreda was elected abbess of the double monastery, which despite its bleak location was a rich and royally endowed establishment. Despite this she lived a life of great holiness and simplicity:

> It is told of her that from the time of her entering the monastery, she would never wear any linen but only woollen garments, and would seldom wash in a hot bath, unless just before the greater festivals, as Easter, Whitsuntide, and the Epiphany, and then she did it last of all, when the other handmaids of Christ who were there had been washed, served by her and her attendants. (Bede 4: 19)

Etheldreda rarely ate more than once per day, except at the greater festivals, or out of urgent necessity. She also remained at prayer in the church through the small hours from matins until dawn, unless ill.

At midsummer in the year 679, Etheldreda found a tumour growing on her neck. She believed this to be punishment for wearing elaborate jewellery of gold and pearls when she was young. The surgeon at the monastery lanced the boil and she recovered briefly for a few days. Sadly, death took her on 23 June, just seven years after she founded the abbey.

Respecting her wishes, Etheldreda was buried as a good Christian, wrapped in a plain shroud in a simple grave, without jewels or any other possessions.

Her sister Seaxburga, the widow of the King of Kent, succeeded her as abbess and, sixteen years after the burial, she decided to move Etheldreda's body into a stone coffin inside the monastery. She sent the monks to look for some stone and they found a Roman-style white marble coffin at Grantchester. A tent was erected over the open grave:

> and all the congregation, the brothers on the one side, and the sisters on the other, standing about it singing, while the abbess, with a few others, had gone within to take up and wash the bones, on a sudden we heard the abbess within cry out with a loud voice, 'Glory be to the name of the Lord.'

The body of this pious nun, this good Christian was found to be uncorrupted … proof of her virginity. Miracles began to happen around the body. If the linen of her gown was touched it could expel demons and cure diseases. If her old coffin was touched it could cure pain and dimness of the eyes. The monastery now began to enjoy being the subject of pilgrims wishing to pray at the shrine of St Etheldreda.

The shrine lay undisturbed, a place of miracles and worship with monks watching over the tomb, saying their prayers, contemplating in the chapter house, working the land around, eating their meagre meals and chanting, for 100 years … until the time of the Viking raids when many monks and nuns were slaughtered. One raised an axe to break into Etheldreda's tomb to steal money that he believed it contained. He made a hole in the tomb and his eyes were torn out of his head.

Time passed and, in approximately 850, the Archpriest decided on Etheldreda's feast day to investigate whether Bede had been right about her. He was advised by a priest against it, who told of the Viking raid and of the miracles. He got four men to help him and they gathered around the tomb.

The Archpriest then started poking a stick through the hole made by the Vikings and to subject the relics to further indignities. It is said that his wife and children promptly died of plague and he moved away from the area only to die shortly after. Two of his accomplices also died, one went mad and the fourth became seriously ill but recovered after he prayed to the saint.

In the late tenth century, the abbey church was extended and refounded and the shrine of St Etheldreda was enlarged to include the bodies of not just Etheldreda but also her sister Seaxburga, Seaxburga's daughter Ermenhilda, and Withburga, a younger sister. Withburga's body was, at that time, in a shrine at East Dereham in Norfolk, close to a healing well.

Withburga's body was stolen in 974, when Brithnoth, Abbot of Ely led a party of armed men to Dereham and threw a great feast. Having got the people of Dereham drunk, he and his men took the saint's body and fled, reaching Brandon by the time that the outraged citizens of Dereham caught up with them. The thieves then leapt into a boat and set sail, while the men of Dereham gave chase along the banks and threw spears, darts and arrows at them. They got away safely, and reached Turbutsey (Queen Adelaide) where they continued the rest of the journey back to the monastery, over land.

The new shrine, which included images of all four 'blessed virgins' in wood overlaid with gold and silver and decorated with precious jewels, was a favourite place for Canute to celebrate the feast of the purification (see the Canute stories in Chapter 7).

Etheldreda's shrine suffered during the reign of William the Conqueror (see the tale of Hereward in Chapter 7) but remained important to Ely with a major fair being held on the three days either side of the feast day. People would buy necklaces (or ribbons) made of silk to represent Bricstans chains (see the story of Bricstan, below). These ribbons were also venerated as having touched her shrine.

Etheldreda's name also became shortened firstly to Aldreda, then changed by the Normans to St Awdrey or Audry. Over time the ribbons sold at Ely became known as St Awdry laces, or even 'tawdry laces'. Spenser and Shakespeare mentioned the latter and Drayton called them 'tawdries, a kind of necklace worn by country wenches'.

During the reign of Henry VIII and the dissolution of the monasteries, Etheldreda's shrine was dismantled and found to contain just a plain stone instead of a white marble coffin. Despite this, the official records of the royal treasury indicate that some 361 ounces of gold were taken from the shrine.

One of Etheldreda's hands was rescued from the sacking of the shrine. It is said that a monk smuggled it away and that it remained hidden until about 1811 when the Duke of Norfolk, whilst carrying out renovations at Arundel Castle in Sussex, discovered a priest hole in which the reliquary had been safely hidden.

The hand, which was described at the time as being 'perfectly entire and quite white' was fitted on a silver spike rising from a circular silver plate, within a bell-shaped ivory case on an ebony stand with ivory ball supports.

In 1953, the relic arrived back in Ely. Today the hand, now dark brown from exposure to the air, is displayed in a glass reliquary behind the font at St Etheldreda's Church in Ely.

BRICSTAN OF CHATTERIS

During the reign of Henry I, in about 1115, there lived in Chatteris a moderately wealthy man named Bricstan. Short in stature, and rather plump, he was kind and generous and had brought up his family to be independent, and never to meddle in the affairs of others. That saying, he also helped those in need, including lending money, for which he sometimes required security, though he never charged interest.

It so happened that Bricstan fell ill and the people feared for his life. He had enjoyed a good life and did not want it to end, so he prayed to God that if he were saved he would become a monk under the rule of St Benedict in the abbey at Ely.

God granted Bricstan's wish and he recovered his health, and being a man of his word he pledged himself and all he had to the convent dedicated to St Etheldreda, and his offer was gratefully accepted.

But word of Bricstan's actions spread to the ears of an evil man named Robert Malart, who was a servant of the king. Malart came to the abbey and accused Bricstan of being a thief. He said Bricstan had found some treasure, which was by right of the law the king's money, and that he had also made money from charging interest on loans, which was a crime known as usury. Bricstan only wanted to become a monk, Malart said, to avoid a prison sentence.

The pious man was arrested and brought to trial at Huntingdon. Here he was tried by Ralph Bassett, a severe judge who had a reputation for imposing severe sentences. At an assize in Leicester, Bassett had sentenced eighty prisoners to hanging and condemned six others to horrible torture.

Many notable men attended Bricstan's trial, including the Bishop of Ely, the Abbot of Ramsey, the Abbot of Thorney and a number of clerks and monks. Bricstan appeared with his wife and pleaded not guilty, for he could not confess to what he had not done. He repeatedly said, 'My Lord God Almighty knows that I speak the truth,' and despite the fact that his wife also supported him, the trial proved to be a mockery, and he was condemned by false witnesses.

And so it was that the innocent man was stripped of his goods, including the sixteen pence and two rings that he carried on him, and was bound and carried in custody to London where he was thrown into a gloomy dungeon.

In this dark dungeon, weighed down with heavy chains and subject to cold and hunger, Bricstan prayed ceaselessly to St Etheldreda, in whose monastery he had wanted to spend the rest of his life, and to St Benedict, whose rule he wished to live under.

One night, when Bricstan was at his most despairing, as he had received no food for three days, he sorrowfully repeated his prayers and at once there appeared in front of him a blaze of light in which he saw St Benedict and St Etheldreda, with her sister Seaxburga. Benedict laid his hands on the chains around the prisoner's feet and they clattered to the ground.

The noise disturbed the guards, who came running to investigate, and who in turn vouched for the miracle to Queen Matilda. She then sent Ralph Bassett, the same man who had doomed Bricstan to his fate, to the dungeon. Bassett was changed by the sight of Bricstan, and by what he heard, and he gladly escorted him to the queen, who ordered the bells to be rung in all the monasteries throughout the city.

The queen also asked if she could keep the chains but Bricstan took them back with him to Ely, where they were hung above the high altar in remembrance of the miracle. Bricstan himself was received in splendour by the whole convent of monks of Ely. A thanksgiving service was held and he was given the monastic habit he had so long desired.

It is said that when Ralph Bassett died he gave a strip of land and ten fat oxen for the maintenance of a monk at an abbey in some part of England – a final act of atonement, perhaps, for his harsh ways.

Whilst researching this story, I came across a reference to a legal case between Robert Malart and Bricstan in the reign of Henry I, the year 1116, with the addition of the following note:

> Bricstan, a man of some means, having applied for admission into the order of monks at Thorney Abbey, the fact comes to the ears of Robert Malart, with the following result : viz., Malart accuses him before the monks of crimes; he is brought to trial before Ralph Basset (the justiciar), and abbots, clerks, and monks, and is convicted.

This reference implies that Bricstan tried to join the monastic order at Thorney Abbey; however, all the other references to the case state that he tried to become a monk at Ely.

Readers may be interested to know that the name of Bricstan has been preserved in Chatteris as the name of a meeting room at the rear of the Church of St Peter and St Paul in Market Hill.

Concerning Bricstan's amazing recovery from death that set him on the path to becoming a monk, a similar miracle happened at Eldernell near Whittlesey in the sixteenth century.

It was a bitterly cold morning in late October, (the Monday before the feast of St Simon and St Jude) and Robert Whyt lay on his bed in Whittlesey, close to death. His friends had gathered round him and the vicar from St Mary's had been called to perform the last rites. Robert was intently praying to Our Lady and was in some sort of trance, when he suddenly got up and walked bareheaded and barefoot to Eldernell, three miles from his home. The vicar and many of his neighbours followed Robert, carrying burning tapers in their hands.

For some time Robert was unable to speak, but on reaching his destination, and in great pain, he called out, 'Our Lady, help.' The vicar and the neighbours then saw tears streaming from the eyes of the statue of Our Blessed Lady, and noted that Robert immediately began to recover his health.

Eldernell Chapel was consecrated to Our Lady in 1525. It contained an image of the Blessed Virgin, which is said to have wrought the above miracle. The chapel fell into disrepair after the dissolution of the monasteries and was eventually demolished. The account was written down by Roger Dodynton, a Thorney monk.

The base of what is likely to have been a stone cross sits at the corner of The Avenue and Causeway Close in the town of March. It has a number of theories connected to it. I personally prefer the following story.

The Devil, the Church and the Stone Cross

A long time ago, long before the Fens were drained, the town of March was part of the parish of Doddington and, as such, the people had to walk or ride five miles to the far end of the island to get to church each Sunday.

So the people decided to build their own church on a site part way between Town End and Merchford, and they hired the best draughtsmen and stone masons to construct the new place of worship.

But often in the mornings, when the workers came to continue their work, they found that the progress they had made the previous day had been undone, and they had to start over again.

This carried on for many weeks, whilst the people speculated on what was happening. Some said it was the work of the creatures who lived in the water, others that it was demons that lived in the air, and yet others that it was the Devil himself.

The people's speculation was answered one night when a young man was making his way home from an evening drinking with friends at Merchford to his home not far from the new church site. This young man, as he approached the building site, heard strange sounds coming from the building, and smelt a strange sulphurous smell. He looked over and also saw some mysterious lights emanating from behind the stone wall.

Being as they say 'one over the eight' the lad decided to go to investigate what was happening. As he clambered around the piles of stones, he was startled by two little creatures like demons, with long tails, running past him screeching.

Not deterred, the young man carried on through the door opening and into the nave where he saw two red eyes glaring at him and he heard the demonic laugh as the Devil himself started to move towards him.

In a fit of panic, he rushed out of the church as fast as his feet would carry him, but suddenly, unable to see his way in the darkness, he tripped over a piece of stone and fell flat down onto the ground as the Devil flew over him.

The next thing the young man knew he was being woken up the following morning by the builders arriving to start work. He told them his tale and they went to see the local clergy, who decided to move the church to its present site at Town End. To protect the old site from the Devil, they built a stone cross to scare him away.

The base of the stone cross can still be seen just down the road from the marvellous St Wendreda's Church. In the first half of the twentieth century, children used to walk around the top step of the 'stone cross' twelve times and then listen carefully to hear the Devil sharpening his knives.

There are a number of similar stories connected to churches in Cambridgeshire.

The church at Great Paxton was originally planned to be built near the river, but each night the stones were moved to another site and, in time, it was decided to build the church where it now stands.

In Thriplow, the people once planned to build the church in the hollow where the rest of the village stands, but as work was carried out, the stones were moved mysteriously to the top of the hill overlooking the village, which is were it now stands.

In Cottenham, the church is sited at the end of the long village. At one time, the people tried to rebuild it in the centre of the village, but each night the stones were moved to the old site, so the work was abandoned.

Within the county there can also be found the place name 'Sunken Church Field'. Such sites are often linked to the remains of Roman villas, but to the people in the past, the fact that they knew there were the remains of brick or stone buildings beneath the ground often prompted the story of how there had once been a church on the site, but it had sunk into what was then believed to have been marshy ground.

Such a place can be found on the Cambridgeshire/Essex border at Hadstock, and over in the south of Cambridgeshire at Great Abington. Regarding the latter, Enid Porter found an informant who said that the field (which is presently on land belonging to Abington Park Farm) contains the buried ruins of an ancient church. They explained that people would avoid the field at night, but if they did go there and put their ear to the ground, they would hear a spectral choir singing. Sometimes people would also hear the sound of bells ringing deep under the ground.

In the village of Litlington, just north of the old Icknield Way, there used to be a strip of land that has always been known as Heaven's Walls and, like at Abington, local children would not go near it after dark because it was said to be haunted. Later excavations revealed a walled Roman cemetery.

The Mystery of the Whirlin' Cakes

In 1789 an entry was placed in the *Gentleman's Magazine*, by Matthew Harrison of Wisbech, as follows:

> At several villages in the vicinity of Wisbech, in the Isle of Ely, the fifth Sunday in Lent has been, time immemorial, commemorated by the name of Whirlin Sunday, when cakes are made by almost every family, and from the day are called whirlin cakes; but notwithstanding my frequent enquiries, I have not been able to discover the reason of this festival, which, I believe, obtains in no other place in the kingdom, and should be happy if any of your correspondents could elucidate a matter grossly involved in obscurity. I write whirlin as it sounds in my ear … I was going to say that whirlin is

probably a corruption of whirlwind, and that the observance of the Sunday is to perpetuate the remembrance of such a convulsion of Nature having happened in an unusual manner in the village above mentioned; but the supposition is forbidden by the inhabitants considering the day as a festival, as I have already taken notice.

It does not appear to have been a response to this request, but in 1884 the item was copied into 'a classified collection of the chief contents' of the magazine under the title 'Popular Superstitions' by George Gomme. Six years later, Mr Lawrence from Hammersmith wrote to *Fenland Notes & Queries* that:

It is many years now since I was at Leverington, but I well remember that it used to be the custom at the feast then to make Whirlwind cakes. There was a curious old folklore legend attached to this custom. It was to the effect that while a certain old lady of Leverington was one day making cakes for the purpose of entertaining her guests at the feast, the devil came to her, and creating a whirlwind carried her off over the church steeple. In commemoration of this improbable event the custom had grown of making Whirlwind cakes.

A short while later, the Revd Frederick Carylon, vicar of Leverington, confirmed that Whirling Sunday was in mid-Lent and that:

None of the old people know anything of the origin of the Legend. But there are still many who recollect when there was a regular pleasure fair held in Leverington on Whirling Sunday, when a particular kind of whirling cake was made in most houses, and sports of all kinds, especially boxing matches, were carried on, and a regular holiday observed. There was no religious ceremony that I can hear of observed on the day beyond the ordinary Church Services. Whirling cakes still continue to be made in one or two houses, but that and the memory of the day only remain. The Legend of the old woman being whirled over the church steeple is still repeated.

Antiquarians in the nineteenth century pointed out that in other parts of the country, the fifth Sunday in Lent is known as Carling or Careling Sunday and that dishes of peas cooked in butter were eaten. They speculate that Whirling Sunday is just a local variant of this tradition.

But the story of the woman and the Devil must have evolved from somewhere. Wouldn't it be nice to know what event prompted the story and what other parishes commemorated the Sunday? It would also be really good to have the recipe for whirling cakes!

7

OF KINGS
AND CASTLES

This chapter contains a number of tales that might be described as histories, as they describe historical figures and events. The other tales are folk stories that have grown around the histories. The first set of tales are about the famous King Canute (Cnut) who seems to have been a popular figure in the county, and is even supposed to have authorised the founding of the town of Littleport. This is followed by the tale of Osbert Fitz Hugh and Wandlebury, and then the varied tales of Hereward the Saxon. The tales that evolved around the loss of the treasure of King John are then explored, and the section concludes with a number of local tales from the English Civil War.

KING CANUTE AND THE FENS

The most common tale of King Canute the Great is of how he showed that he could not control the waves. Much lesser known are the tales of his time in the Fens. It seems appropriate to explore some of them.

After Canute's success at the Battle of Assendun on St Luke's Day 1016, he began ruling most of the kingdom, but with the death of

Edmund 'Ironside' on 30 November, he became ruler of a unified English kingdom as part of his North Sea Empire, which also included Norway, Denmark and part of Sweden. He was just 23 years of age, and was to rule for another nineteen years.

One of his first actions was to build a church near to the battle site at Hadstock, on the border of Cambridgeshire and Essex, to commemorate those who had been killed on both sides.

The king soon became known for his patronage of storytellers, poets and minstrels, but he was also a writer of poetry and song himself. The *Liber Eliensis* (*Book of Ely*) explains how one song was inspired:

> King Cnut was making his way to Ely by boat, accompanied by Emma, his queen, and the nobles of the kingdom, desiring to celebrate solemnly there, in accordance with custom, the Purification of St Mary … When they were approaching the land, the king rose up in the middle of his men and directed the boatmen to make for the little port at full speed, and then ordered them to pull the boat forward more slowly as it came in. As he turned his eyes towards the church which stood out at a distance, situated as it was at the top

of a rocky eminence, he heard the sound of sweet music echoing on all sides, and, with ears alert, began to drink in the melody more fully the closer he approached. For he realised that it was the monks singing psalms in the monastery and chanting clearly the Divine Hours. He urged the others who were present in the boats to come round about him and sing, joining him in jubilation. Expressing with his own mouth his joyfulness of heart, he composed aloud a song in English, the beginning of which runs as follows:

> *Merry sung the monks within Ely*
> *When Canute the King was rowing by;*
> *Row, my men, near the land,*
> *And hear we these monks' song.*

Canute's affection for Ely can also be seen in the tale of how, once again, he was travelling there to celebrate the feast of the Purification (Candlemas – 2 February) but the weather was very severe and the waterways were frozen. The king's advisers suggested that he keep the holy feast at another house of God, because to reach the abbey he would have to cross the treacherous Fens, where the danger of drowning under broken ice was very real.

But the king was determined to get to Ely somehow and asked for a volunteer who would like to walk ahead of his wagon across Soham Mere, which was then an immense body of water. None of his men came forward, as they all feared crossing the mere, but one standing in the crowd, a certain large and rugged man named Brithmar, stepped forward. This stout man, whose surname was Budde, on account of his bulk, was a local man and familiar with its waters.

The crowd watched as Brithmar spoke to the king and offered to go before him across the frozen waters. Without delay Brithmar went ahead and King Canute the Great followed him in the wagon at a fast pace. Behind the king came his followers, one by one, with gaps in between; and they all safely crossed the frozen mere, except perhaps for the odd bruise from slipping and falling on the ice.

After Canute had kept the festival, he rewarded Brithmar by granting perpetual freedom for him and his sons to enjoy their land holdings. Canute was also generous to the ordinary Fenland people, and enabled the allocation of common pasture land on the marshes:

> King Canute gave by command by Turkhill the Dane that to every village standing about the Fens there should be set out a several marsh. Who so divided that ground that each village should have so much of the marsh as of the firm ground of each touched of that lying close against it. And he ordained that the pasture in the marsh should lie common for the preservation of peace among them.

It is also said that Canute built a hunting lodge at Bodsey near Ramsey and that he would reach this by crossing Whittlesey Mere. Many also recalled that Canute's sons travelled across the mere on their way to their schooling at Peterborough Abbey.

One day, when the sons and servants of Canute were sailing across Whittlesey Mere, and were singing and laughing under the sail, the winds suddenly grew strong:

> At once, a turbulent storm arose that enclosed them on every side so that laying aside all hope they were in utter despair of their life. But such was the clemency of God that by his providence some of them were delivered safely out of those furious and raging waves. Others, again according to his just and sacred judgement, he permitted ... to pass out of this frail life.

After the storm died down, the king realised that his sons had drowned in the mere and so: 'he ordered his soldier and servants with their swords ... to mark out a certain ditch in the marshes near between Ramsey and Whittlesey and afterwards that workmen and labourers should cleanse them'.

The causeway that the soldiers prepared with their swords became known as King's Dyke.

The fact that the latter story stayed in people's memories is indicated by the following entry, which appeared in the *Cambridge Independent* press in February 1913:

> Two tiny coffins have recently been found in the monastic burial ground of Peterborough, and have been placed in Peterborough Cathedral. One is 2ft 6ins in length, and the other 2ft 8ins. They are said locally to be the coffins of the twin children of King Canute (955-1035), who were drowned in Whittlesey Mere as they were crossing to be educated at Peterborough Abbey.

Another story concerning Canute was told to Barrett by Chafer Legge and included in *Tales from the Fens*. Chafer said that the man called Legres in the tale was one of his ancestors. This is my version of the tale.

The founding of Littleport

One day while travelling across the Fens, King Canute decided that he wanted to spend some time alone fishing. He dressed as a common man, prepared a boat for the journey, and then set off, leaving his men in their camp.

Not long after he had set off, the weather changed from bright sun to grey clouds and rain, and Canute decided that he should leave the boat and find somewhere to shelter. It so happened that there was a fisherman's hut nearby and Canute knocked at the door and asked if he could come in out of the rain.

Legres, the man who answered the door, was poor, but he had a warm fire, and he offered the visitor a horn of ale and some delicious eel stew. The two men chatted for a while and then went back outside to see what the weather was doing.

The day was still stormy and night was beginning to fall, so the king asked Legres if he could lead him to a nearby monastery where he could get lodgings for the night. The fisherman escorted the king to the monastery but, much to their surprise, Canute was turned away by the drunken monk who answered the door.

The king was angry but Legres said that he was not at all surprised by the reception. He said that the monks were not likely to be in a fit state until late the next morning, and added that he would be happy to have a guest in his hut for the night.

The king accepted the invitation and the two returned to the hut where they drank a few more horns of ale and Legres told the story of his life.

Eventually Legres came to tell the king of how his wife had been carried off and raped by the monks and how he had been flogged for attempting to rescue her. He also explained how those same monks set their vicious dogs on them as they made their escape.

As the tale continued, the king learnt how the wife of Legres had died soon after the rape, and since that time, every year on his son's birthday, Legres had killed a monk, making it look like they had drowned in the marsh, and with each death he added a notch to a willow stick. There were now eighteen notches.

Well, the king and Legres settled down for the night but the fleas in the bedding made the king itch so much that he went outside, and seeing that the weather had eased, he wrapped himself in his cloak and slept in the bottom of his boat.

The next morning, as the sun was rising, the king woke up to the sound of splashing near the boat. He peered over the side and saw a beautiful girl bathing in the water. He watched as the girl finished bathing and he then saw her put on the clothing of a boy and dirty her face. She then walked to the fisherman's hut, opened the door and went in. Canute then realised that Legres had a daughter, rather than a son.

Canute also realised that the disguise was the way that Legres was protecting his daughter from being attacked by the monks and decided that something should be done about the situation.

Later that day, Canute took Legres to meet his men and they decided to punish the monks for not behaving like the men of God they were meant to be. They marched to the monastery and forced their way in. A number of monks were killed and the others were made to build a little town with nice houses in which Legres and his daughter, who were granted their freedom, and the king's protection, could live.

And so Littleport was constructed on land five miles north of Ely, with a port, a mill, a brewery and an inn, and Legres the fisherman was elected as the first mayor of the town.

The following story was recorded by Gervase of Tilbury in his *Recreation for an Emperor (Otia Imperialia)*. This early thirteenth-century book contained a selection of 'wonders', collected by Gervase, who is believed to have been born in West Tilbury, Essex. Gervase was a relative of King Henry II and, as such, was well travelled and connected to the courts of a number of monarchs, including Otto IV Holy Roman Emperor, to whom his book was dedicated.

The tale is focused around Wandlebury hillfort in the Gog Magog hills, south-east of Cambridge (an area featured earlier in this book).

THE PROWESS OF OSBERT FITZ HUGH

In England, near the boundary of the diocese of Ely, there is a town named Cambridge. In its territory, not far from the town, there is a place called Wandlebury ... Now in the place, on top of a slight hill ... there is a plateau enclosed by a circle of earthworks, with a single entrance, like a gate.

There is an ancient tradition, that if a knight enters this plateau at the dead of night, when the moon is shining, and cries 'Knight to knight, come forth,' immediately he will be confronted by a warrior, armed and ready to fight, who, charging horse to horse, either overthrows his opponent or is overthrown himself.

But the warrior must enter the enclosure alone, though there is no reason why his companions cannot look on from outside. As proof of the truth of this I quote a story told to me by the country people of the neighbourhood.

There was once, not long ago, a most gallant and virtuous knight, second to few among knights in power and inferior to none in prowess. His name was Osbert, son of Hugh, or Osbert Fitz Hugh.

One day Osbert came as a guest to the town I have mentioned, and, it being winter time, after dinner, as is the fashion among the nobility, the household gathered around the fireside. Here they would tell, and listen to tales of the deeds of the people of old.

In time the wondrous tale mentioned before came to be described by one of the company. Osbert, on hearing this, resolved to test by experience, the truth of the tale he had heard. So he chose one of his noble squires and they set off for the place called Wandlebury.

On arriving at the spot mentioned, Osbert, clad in chain mail, mounted his steed, dismissed his squire and entered the camp alone.

Osbert then cried aloud 'Knight to knight, come forth,' and no sooner had he called than a knight, or what looked like a knight, came rapidly towards him, similarly armed.

Well, they both put up their shields, aimed their lances, and charged towards each other. They exchanged blows, and Osbert having avoided the spear thrust of his adversary, powerfully knocked his opponent to the ground.

The other knight fell, but was soon on his feet again, and, seeing that Osbert was leading off his horse by the bridle, as the spoils of the fight, he hurled his lance, like a javelin, piercing Osbert's thigh.

Our knight however, in the joy of his victory, either did not feel or chose to ignore the wound, and emerged from the field victorious, whilst his adversary disappeared. He gave the horse which he had taken as spoils to his squire. It was large in stature, sprightly and very handsome to behold.

On his return, Osbert was met by members of the household, who marvelled at his tale, rejoiced at the fall of the defeated knight and praised his valour.

When Osbert took off his armour he saw that one of his boots was filled with clotted blood. The family were shocked at the wound, but the knight dismissed their fears.

Word of the deed had spread and the townsfolk, aroused from slumber, gathered round to see the horse, proof of the triumph. Its eyes were wild, its neck stiff and its coat black. The knight's saddle and saddle cloth were also black.

As soon as the cock crowed, the horse, bucking violently, foaming at the nostrils, and pounding the earth with its hooves, burst the reins that held it and regained its freedom. It took flight, and though some set off in pursuit, it was soon lost to sight.

And our noble knight had a permanent reminder of the wound he had sustained, such that every year, on the anniversary of that night, at the very same moment of the occurrence, the wound, though healed over on the surface, would open again.

So it came to pass, that the distinguished knight, some years later, crossed the sea, and, after performing many deeds of courage against the infidel, gave his life and his soul to God.

Research indicates that Osbert Fitz Hugh may have been the founder of a priory at Westwood, Droitwich. He is also mentioned in medieval charters of the 1130s and 1140s.

His tale includes a number of common motifs – a fairy horse, fights between heroes and demons, and a wound that breaks open every year. Such fights are often found in Nordic legends and the latter is in the Arthurian legends.

Glenys Goetinck noted that the story resembles a twelfth-century tale in *Lay of the Thorn* (*Lai de l'Espine*). In this tale, an encounter takes place at a ford on St John's Eve in which the hero unhorses his adversary and takes the horse away with him. Glenys also remarked on the similarity between the Wandlebury legend and the Welsh tales of Peredur, and of Owein. In the former, the hero is told:

> Go to the top of the mountain and there thou wilt see a bush. And at the foot of the bush there is a slab. Ask three times for a man to come and joust … Peredur went on his way and came alongside the bush and asked for a man to joust with him. And a black man rose from under the slab with a bony horse under him and huge rusty armour, on him and his horse. They fought, and as Peredur would throw the black man to the ground he would leap back into his saddle. And Peredur dismounted and drew his sword and at that moment the black man disappeared with Peredur's horse and his own, so that he did not see him again.

Many people, when asked about the Fens, think of Hereward the Wake, and indeed the fame of this character grew immensely with the publication of the novel of the same name by Charles Kingsley in 1866. Kingsley was Professor of Modern History at Cambridge University from 1860–69 and had used his knowledge of the area to enhance the book.

I have constructed the following version of the tale from not just Kingsley's book but also the various historical accounts. I have also chosen to disregard the addition of Wake to Hereward's name as it appears to have been introduced in later medieval times, when the Wake family took over lands in Lincolnshire and wanted to enjoy the benefits of a noble lineage. The tale contains a number of storytelling motifs, particularly from the northern European traditions.

HEREWARD THE SAXON

When Hereward, the son of Leofric of Bourne in Lincolnshire, was young, it did not seem as if he was going to follow in his father's footsteps as a good and reliable leader. The young man much preferred the company of those who were just a little 'wild' and was proud of his Danish 'Viking' ancestry.

So when the 18-year-old Hereward was caught stealing from his own family, Leofric managed to persuade King Edward the Confessor to make the young man an outlaw, and banish him from the kingdom.

This action seems not to have been regarded by the young man as a punishment, but rather as a way of exploring the world – and he soon started to attract fame. Tales were told of how he (accompanied by his servant Martin Lightfoot) helped damsels in distress, wrestled with bears (and giants) and defeated brave warriors in hand-to-hand combat in Ireland, Cornwall and Flanders.

And so it was that Hereward was a soldier of fortune in Flanders when King Edward died and the succession to the throne was challenged by William (the Conqueror) at the Battle of Hastings. When Hereward heard that the victorious Normans had seized his father's estates he returned to England, where he found the head of his brother on a pole outside the great hall. He was also informed that his brother had been killed protecting the family property.

Hereward then found out that the Norman invaders were enjoying a feast in the great hall, and he determined to wreak revenge. He asked Martin Lightfoot to wait outside the door with his sword drawn, ready to kill anyone who tried to escape, then he forced open the door, drew his sword and rushed into the hall. He killed fourteen Normans and the remainder who tried to escape were killed by Martin.

The two men were now outlaws, but before they took any further action, Hereward wanted to be knighted, and not at the instigation of a Norman. He went to Peterborough Abbey where his uncle was abbot and got him to carry out the request.

The news spread that Hereward was now in England, and he was asked to become the leader of a band of English and Danish warriors who were camped at Ely. He took a ship from the coast of Lincolnshire, down the Well Stream between the ancient sea banks towards Wisbech and on to Upwell and finally to the Isle of Ely. Here he was welcomed by the monks, particularly Thurston, the abbot of Ely, and swore fealty at the shrine of St Etheldreda.

Hereward then heard the news that his uncle had died and that the Norman Bishop Turold, who had fought alongside William at Hastings, was to be the new abbot of Peterborough. The rebels sailed to the city and removed the plate of silver and gold, and the precious books, before setting fire to the abbey. The Danes took away the hoard for safekeeping.

By this time, word of the rebellion came to the attention of King William, who led his army to Ely, but the Fens at this time were an ideal place to hold a siege, as neither food nor fresh water was a problem.

The chroniclers described the area as being rich in not just eels but also burbots, lampreys, perch, pickerels, pike, roach, salmon and sturgeon, along with beasts of the chase (deer, fox and rabbit). There was also an abundance of wildfowl – coots, didappers, ducks, geese, herons, teal and watercrows. The island was also easy to defend, being surrounded by treacherous marshes.

King William decided to construct castles and fortifications around the Fens from which he could build causeways to cross the marshes, but he was repeatedly outwitted by Hereward and his men. On the first attempt, William got his men to build a causeway of great pieces of timber, stone and faggots fastened underneath with cowhides. But this was not strong enough to bear the weight of the Norman soldiers and many of them drowned in the marsh. One man managed to reach the Isle of Ely. His name was Deda and he was allowed to stay in Ely to see the strength of the English resistance before being encouraged to return to William to suggest that the king make peace.

The king was seriously tempted to negotiate peace until one of his men, Ivo Taillebois, said that he knew of a French witch who was skilled at making powerful curses and carrying out rituals that they could use to dispel the enemy. William told Ivo to summon the witch, whilst he kept up the blockade of the Isle of Ely.

Hereward, wondering what the Normans were planning next, and knowing that William and his soldiers were camped at Brandon, trimmed his hair and beard and, in disguise, rode there on his trusty old mare, Swallow. The horse was a lean, ill-shaped creature but swift and nimble in its paces. On the way to Brandon, Hereward met a potter, who agreed to lend him his pots. In this way

Hereward got safely into the Norman camp, where he displayed and sold some of the pots, and listened to the Normans' plans. He was briefly recognised but managed to escape to Somersham.

By this time William's men had gathered the materials to build another causeway from Aldreth. Hereward, yet again in disguise, became one of the fishermen who volunteered to help. He waited until nightfall and then set fire to all the equipment.

On the next occasion, William increased the security before ordering his men to commence building a new causeway with a tower in the middle, for the newly arrived French witch to use for her rituals. Eight days later, the rebels, carefully hidden in the reeds, watched as the French witch climbed up to the top of the tower and started to use spells, rituals and curses designed to scare them.

The Norman soldiers were lined up on the causeway to watch the proceedings. They did not at first notice when Hereward and his men set fire to the vegetation and loosed arrows at them, until many of them were struck and others fell to their deaths in the marsh. With the tower burning beneath the witch, she fell and broke her neck.

After this experience, William decided to use different tactics. The first was to punish the monks at Ely by seizing their lands until they had paid taxes that were imposed upon them. The monks fled from Ely to Bottisham, taking the treasures of the abbey, and it is said that when they went to hand over 700 marks in silver to the king (which would weigh about 400 pounds and be worth about £400 at that time) they were one-eighth of an ounce short.

The king, they say, lost his temper and demanded another 300 marks from the monks, who begged him for mercy. He took no pity on them and insisted that they must pay or they would not get their lands back. The monks, when they discovered that William had stolen treasure that they had hidden in secret places, realised that they had no choice but to burn the precious statues of the Four Blessed Virgins (including St Etheldreda) and a life-size image of the Madonna and Child in order to melt off the gold leaf.

Eventually, the demoralised monks led the Norman soldiers to the abbey at Ely where they attacked and captured many of the rebels. Hereward, however, escaped with a few men by hiding in the bottom of a boat, and made his way to Upwell.

As he left the marshland, Hereward killed his trusty steed who was no longer able to serve him. He did not want the French to get her and so, as she was swimming behind the boat, he cut the rope and left her to the watery wastes.

At about this time it seems that Hereward was losing his support. It had been too long since the Battle of Hastings and William had now secured the throne, so that few men wanted to join the rebels. The Danish also tired of the struggle and returned home, taking some of the Peterborough treasure with them.

It is said that Hereward continued to resist the Normans and, while mounting an attack on Stamford in Lincolnshire, he and his men found themselves hopelessly lost in Rockingham Forest. A story tells of how St Peter sent a white wolf to guide the rebels to safety and, when darkness fell, burning lights appeared on every man's lance and on every tree, and they soon found their way to safety. Hereward took the sign from St Peter as an appreciation for his actions in rescuing the treasure of the abbey of Peterborough many years earlier.

The accounts of Hereward's later life are conflicting. It seems that he eventually made peace with William and was allowed to live in comfort. However, he had other enemies and one day, whilst he was resting, sixteen Normans entered his home. Hereward, using his trusty sword 'Brainbiter' and his lance, killed fifteen of the attackers and finally dispatched the remainder using his shield, but four more knights arrived and stabbed him with their spears.

So Hereward the hero died fighting, and it is said that his body was taken by barge to be buried in the Church of St Guthlac at Crowland, in the choir area next to the high altar.

And on by Porsad and by Asendyke,
By winding reaches on, and shining meres

Between gray reed-ronds and green alder-beds,
A dirge of monks and wail of women rose
In vain to Heaven for the last Englishman;
Then died far off within the boundless mist,
And left the Norman master of the land.

In a lecture in Wisbech in 1868 Jonathan Peckover noted that the local stories of Hereward had almost died away in this country. Similarly, W.H. Barrett, in the introductory material to his *More Tales from the Fens*, argued that as the tale of Hereward is not within the oral tradition in the Littleport area, it may have been made up by the clergy. He said that if the story had been true, then Norman skeletons should have been found by dyke diggers who would have connected the finds to the tale.

The twelfth-century 'Deeds of Hereward the Saxon' (*De Gestis Herewardi Saxonis*) by Richard of Ely did, however, describe how fishermen had dredged up Norman skeletons in rusty armour in the area.

In the thirteenth century people would also visit a wooden castle in the Fens known as Hereward's Castle. At this time, it seems that Hereward was a character recognised throughout East Anglia and the East Midlands.

The common belief is that William the Conqueror's causeway was constructed at a place called Alrehede, which is generally believed to be from Aldreth to Haddenham, and indeed there is evidence for an ancient earthwork at the junction of the old fen causeway and Iram Drove, south of Aldreth. Known as Belsar's Hill, this circular earthwork is the potential site of a fort built by William to attack Ely.

However, archaeological evidence was found in the 1930s that might indicate that one of the causeways was built from the Island of Stuntney towards Braham Dock to the south-east of Ely. There are ancient earthworks near here and eleventh-century weapons have been recovered from the area, as well as from an old river bed at Quanea (Quaveney). Old maps also show that there was once a waterway in the area known as Hereward's Brook (Herewardisbeche).

This is my adaptation of the tale told to W.H. Barrett by his great-uncle who lived close to Gold Hill, which was included in *Tales from the Fens*. Gold Hill is described as being near the suspension bridge over the Hundred Foot River between Littleport and Welney, and close to an ancient trackway that connected Wisbech and Littleport (A1101).

As the welney.org.uk website points out, the area known as 'Suspension Bridge' hasn't had or been a suspension bridge since 1926; Gold Hill doesn't have gold or a hill; the Hundred Foot Bank is neither a hundred feet high, wide nor long, and is actually one bank of the New Bedford River, otherwise known as the Hundred Foot River, which is tidal but sometimes called a 'drain'. But enough of that … and on to the story.

King John and Wisbech

You will probably have heard of King John, the king with the bad reputation. It is said that he spent too much time in this country and the barons didn't like it, and that he disregarded the laws of the land and the barons didn't like that either.

Well, shortly after the experience of having to sign the Magna Carta at Runnymede in 1215, the king went back on his word, and started to travel around the country collecting all the treasure that he had left in the abbeys for safekeeping. This treasure included the crown of his grandmother, Empress Matilda, the Sword of Tristram and a great weight of gold, silver and precious jewels.

On 9 October 1216 King John arrived at King's Lynn in Norfolk, where he intended to spend a few days not only seizing more of his treasure but also trying some of the fine continental wines that had come into the port. He was also making arrangements to charter a ship to carry this and some of his baggage up to Grimsby in north Lincolnshire, where he was going later.

John, however, tasted far too much of the wine, and when he awoke on the morning of 12 October he could not face the long journey to his next stop at Swineshead in Lincolnshire. Instead he decided to make another stop on his journey at Wisbech Castle, particularly as he had heard that the travelling fair was in the town.

Wisbech had a reputation for its travelling fair, which it was said had the best of entertainments, the best of food and drink, and the finest of young women offering their services. So the king travelled to Wisbech and to the castle, where he safely locked away his belongings and his treasure in a big wooden chest in his bedchamber. He then put the key around his neck, changed into the clothes of a commoner and crossed the bridge to the fair.

The fair was as busy as ever, and the king had an enjoyable day. He tasted the delicious hot chestnuts, drank some of the local cider, watched the fire eaters, jugglers, minstrels and travelling players, and admired the pretty young women.

One particular girl really caught his eye, and he invited her back to his apartment in the castle, where he offered her some of the fine wine he had purchased at King's Lynn. Little did the king know, but each time he poured her some wine the girl would pour some of it back into his goblet, and so as she pretended to be so, the king became drunk and grew drowsy. He dismissed his attendants and asked his guards to wait outside the door. He then asked the girl to accompany him to his bedchamber. The girl agreed to this and, after a short kiss and a cuddle, the king fell asleep and began snoring loudly.

The girl, wide awake and sober, got out of bed and began to explore the room. She saw the big chest in the corner and went back to the king to look for the key, which she found on the cord around his neck.

With some effort the girl managed to get the key from around the king's neck and take it over to the chest where she lifted the heavy lid and admired the treasure. She could barely believe her luck, so much gold, silver and jewels, far too much to resist the temptation to take at least some of it.

The girl started to seriously think. If she could carry enough of the treasure out of the room, she could give up following the fair and spending nights with strangers. She could live somewhere nice and maybe get married, if she could find someone to have her, with her reputation.

Then the girl remembered the stable boy, who she knew worked at the castle, and she hatched a plan and crept to the door of the apartment, where she told the guards that the king wished to see the stable boy at once. The guards, ever fearful of the bad-tempered monarch, did as requested and sent word to the stables for the boy to attend the king. Soon the boy was in the king's bedchamber beside the girl, silently watching King John snoring contentedly.

The stable boy then said to the guards that the king had ordered them to take the rest of the night off to visit the fair. Once again they did not question the order; in fact they were rather pleased to be given the chance to enjoy themselves for once. So the stable boy and the girl, alone aside from the sleeping king, lay their cloaks upon the floor and loaded as much of the gold, silver and precious jewels as they could onto them. They then bundled up the cloaks and carried them out of the door, down the stairs and out into the night. They were soon in the stables where they hid their bundles underneath a pile of hay, and then waited until first light when the muck cart came into the castle.

The job of the muck cart driver was to collect all the muck from the privies and the stables and load it onto his cart. He took off his cloak and hat and set to work. But when he had finished and was just wiping the sweat from his brow, the stable boy came up behind him and slit his throat from ear to ear. The boy then bundled the man into the back of the cart and hid the body under the pile of stinking dung.

The boy then hid the bundles of jewels in the back of the muck cart, picked up the driver's cloak and hat from where they had been discarded, put them on himself and finally climbed onto the cart. The girl hid at his feet as the boy reined in the horses and they set off out of the castle.

Getting out of the castle was simple, as no one ever stops the foul-smelling muck cart, and they were soon on their way out of the town and onto the fen heading east. When they had got far enough away, they rescued the bundles, unhitched the horses and pushed the cart, which included the driver's body, into the river.

They then rode off in the direction of Littleport, along the ancient trackway. However, as they approached Welney they heard the sound of bird calls from within the tall reeds to either side of the causeway. They soon realised that they were surrounded by Fenmen and they could see that the men were suspicious of them being about so early.

The stable lad realised that the best way to survive would be to confess what they had done, to tell the whole story of how they had come by the treasure and to offer some of the jewels to the men, and hope for the best!

Their offer was gratefully accepted by the Fenmen, and the lad and the girl decided to stay with their new friends. They were soon married and moved into a nice little cottage, and the treasure was safely buried in an ancient barrow that later came to be known as Gold Hill. Some say that nine months after the night that the girl spent with the king, a son was born and they named him Prince. He grew up to be the finest thief in the area!

As for King John, when he woke up and realised that much of his treasure was missing, he was furious. It didn't take long for him to work out that the girl and the stable lad were missing and that they must have stolen the treasure – and he sent his guards to search for them.

It is said that the order to search for the treasure has never been retracted and that people are still searching for it today, only they are looking over near the Wash, which is where King John and his baggage train, which is estimated to have been about two miles long, went next on the way to Lincolnshire.

The next part of the story is history, as they say, and as the medieval chronicler Roger of Wendover, in his *Flores Historium* (1220) tells us:

> heading for the north, he [King John] lost by an unexpected accident all the wagons, carts and packhorses with the treasures, precious vessels and all the other things that he cherished with special care: for the ground was opened up in the midst of the waves and bottomless whirlpools engulfed everything, together with men and horses, so that not a single foot soldier got away to bear tidings of the disaster to the king.

History also records that King John died at Newark on 19 October. It was said that his body was stripped of all but his underwear after his death, and that he was buried wrapped in just the robes of the monk who read the last rites. There is also an account by a priest who went to Newark to say a mass for the dead king's soul and subsequently told the Abbot of Coggeshall that he had seen men leaving the city laden with loot!

The people of Lincolnshire also have a tale that King John was poisoned at Swineshead Abbey, and yet others have theorised that the king may have either sold or pawned many of his treasures for ready money to pay the thousands of mercenaries that accompanied and protected him.

But this is all the stuff of debate and not for this book, though I have included the Swineshead incident in my *Lincolnshire Folk Tales* book!

Legends of the English Civil War

Whilst it is a well-known fact that the greylag goose is the only species indigenous to the British Isles and that in former times it bred abundantly in the East Anglian Fens, it is much less known that there was once a 'Brotherhood of the Grey Goose Feather' – a secret society of Fenland people who each carried a split grey goose feather and protected all others who did the same. I would now like to tell one of their stories, namely my adaptation of a couple of tales collected by W.H. Barrett, and printed in his *Tales from the Fens*.

The story fits well with the historical record, as King Charles I did stay at Snowre Hall in Norfolk from 30 April before taking the Southery ferry and crossing the Fens. An account also survives to show that the king stayed at a cottage in the village of Coppingford, just off the Great North Road, a few miles north of Huntingdon on 3 May. He then travelled north to the Scottish camp near Southwell in Nottinghamshire for a meeting on 5 May.

Barrett also heard that the protection of the split grey goose feather was still being used by French prisoners in the early 1800s (see the tale in Chapter 5) and that the tradition was believed by the local people to have survived for hundreds of years, though without written record. Chafer Legge, who told to Barrett the story of Mucky Porter (see 'Grey goose feathers', below), explained that whilst his own father was a member of the brotherhood and knew the secret password, he never passed it on to his son.

The second tale in this section concerns a siege at Woodcroft Castle, near Peterborough, during the Civil War. The story also includes a few lines from a poem by John Clare about the tale. Clare was employed at the age of 12 to drive the plough at the castle, but left the employment as he found it disagreeable to be wading in water up to his knees when the moat overflowed onto the causeway. In his diaries he recorded hearing the story of the siege.

The final part of this section is a set of local anecdotes about Oliver Cromwell. I believe that we need to recognise the fact that for five years he was Lord Protector of England and, as a consequence, should be regarded as one of the most famous men in not just Cambridgeshire but the whole country.

Grey goose feathers

At the end of April 1646, when the Civil War was turning against the Royalists, King Charles escaped from Oxford under cover of darkness, with his good friend John Ashburnham and his chaplain Michael Hudson. They headed for Norfolk and a place of safety, at Snowre Hall, near Downham Market.

They arrived at Snowre Hall where they spent a few days and, during this time, their host Sir Ralph Skipwith discussed with them where they should go next. They were very wary of being captured by the Parliamentarians in the region of Cromwell's home and decided to go around the Fens, through St Ives to Huntingdon and up the Great North Road. From there, they hoped to go to the Scottish camp near Newark to see if the Scotsmen would help the Royalist cause.

For the trip across the Fens, they needed to get the help of a local man who knew the area for, at that time, before drainage, it was very dangerous. Mr Skipwith recommended that the best man for the task was Mucky Porter, the landlord of The Fleece Inn at Southery.

A messenger was sent to speak to Mucky, who agreed to help the king. However, before he was given the task, he was asked for proof of his honesty and reliability. Mucky showed the king a grey goose feather, took out his knife, split it down the middle and informed the king that he was a true Fenman and that all the true folk of the area carried the split grey goose feather. He then gave half of the feather to the king, saying, 'Whilst fishes have scales, and birds have feathers, I will do all I can for you, and so will every other man who belongs to the Brotherhood of the Grey Goose Feather.'

With King Charles and his men all initiated into the brotherhood, they all left Snowre Hall with Mucky early the following morning, to travel across the Fens. The men were in disguise, with the king wearing a grey coat lent to him by Skipwith, and the hat of a commoner.

Mucky proved to be an expert guide and they soon reached the river crossing at St Ives. But the bridge, which had been partially demolished by Cromwell's forces and turned into a drawbridge, was strongly manned by Parliamentarian troops.

When stopped by the guards, Mucky put his hand into his pocket, took out the split grey goose feather and held it for all to see. The king and his men did the same and the guards, who were also Fenmen, allowed the travellers to cross.

Then Mucky helped the king to reach The Bell Tavern in Huntingdon, where they quenched their thirst. In grateful thanks, the king gave his guide a bag of gold in payment, and travelled on his way.

The king and his men then rode for a few miles to the tiny village of Coppingford where they stayed overnight and, the following day being a Sunday, they rested and read prayers before travelling on to Stamford and then to Newark.

Sadly the king failed to negotiate help from the Scots, who handed him over to Parliament. The Civil War continued until eventually he was captured by Cromwell and his men and finally executed in London on 30 January 1649.

It is said that when Cromwell found out that his troops had allowed the king to cross the river at St Ives, he summoned them to him but, on hearing their story, as a Fenman too, he said, 'It is better for a king to escape than for the Fenmen to go back on a man who carries the split goose feather' – and he let them go.

It is also said, in the Fens, that on the night before the execution of the king, Cromwell was sitting with the rest of his generals when a messenger arrived. The messenger produced a split grey goose feather and placed it on the table before Cromwell, saying that the king, as a member of the brotherhood, asks for mercy.

As the story goes, Cromwell's face went white, he dismissed all those around him, and sat long into the night, staring at the feather. As a Fenman, Cromwell knew what he should do, but when morning came he allowed the beheading to take place.

It is said that Cromwell was never the same after this. He brooded and brooded and it was made worse by the fact that when the Fenland members of his army heard about his actions they refused to follow him, threw their grey goose feathers at his feet and returned to their homes.

Cromwell also changed his views on the drainage of the Fens. In his early political career he had supported the Fenmen in their complaints about the drainage, but after the beheading of the king he enabled the work to continue.

Of the men who accompanied the king, John Ashburnham survived the Civil War, the Protectorate, and went on to serve King Charles II as a diplomat, whereas Michael Hudson met a gruesome end, as the following short tale relates.

The siege of Woodcroft Castle

> *Woodcroft thy castle many a story yields,*
> *How drunken rebels scorning flood & fen,*
> *Turned up their horses in thy blooming fields*

John Clare

In June 1648, in the midst of the Civil War, Michael Hudson, the king's chaplain and Rector of Uffington, along with fifteen men were staying at Woodcroft Castle near Helpston. They were instigating attacks against the Parliamentary forces who were pillaging Huntingdonshire.

Word of their actions reached the Parliamentarians and they made haste to reach the castle, where they placed faggots in the moat and breached the outer wall. The siege lasted from morning until evening as the Roundheads progressed from room to room.

Eventually, the only survivor was Dr Hudson, who managed to get to the roof of the tower, followed by half a dozen of the opposing forces. He tried to surrender but they would not accept his offer and forced him over the parapet. In desperation, and pleading for his life, Hudson hung on to a gargoyle, until the officer in charge swung his sword and hacked off Hudson's right hand.

Hudson fell into the moat, and though sorely wounded, managed to struggle to the muddy bank. By this time the attackers had rushed down from the roof, grabbed their pikes and surrounded him. It is said that the final mortal blow to the head was from a servant of the Rector of Castor. It is also said that Hudson's tongue was cut out by a 'low-bred shopkeeper from Stamford' and that it was kept as a trophy for many years.

The tale has also been kept alive as a ghost story, in which screams are heard from the battlements at night along with an anguished voice calling, 'Mercy, mercy', followed by the clash of steel.

Oliver Cromwell – some local gossip

Oliver Cromwell was born in Huntingdon town centre and it is said that when he first saw a tapestry depicting Satan beckoning his imps, he held out his arms towards it and the midwife remarked that, 'He is for the gallows in this world, and the fires of Hell in the next.'

It is also said that when Cromwell was a baby he was taken to visit his uncle at nearby Hinchingbrooke House, where he was snatched from his cradle by a pet monkey and taken up on to the roof.

Another tale relates how little Oliver fell into the River Ouse and was fished out by a Royalist parson who was fishing nearby. Years afterwards, when Cromwell revisited the scenes of his youth with his triumphant army, he met his rescuer and asked the parson if he remembered the occurrence. 'Truly do I,' was the prompt reply, 'and the Lord forgive me, but I wish I'd let thee drown.'

When he was a little older, on another visit to Hinchingbrooke House, the young Oliver Cromwell met Prince Charles Stuart (the future king) and punched him in the face, making his nose bleed.

In adulthood, Cromwell became a devout Puritan, but he died on the anniversary of his victories at Dunbar and Worcester and some say that he had recalled the tapestry he had seen as a baby and had made a contract with the Devil in return for victory.

It was also noted that Cromwell laughed excessively at his victory, as if he had been drunk, and people believed that the achievement was 'contrary to human prudence'. The same fit of laughter also seized Cromwell just before the Battle of Naseby.

As Cromwell was dying, it was reported that a whale (the personal property of the monarch of this land) was seen swimming up the River Thames, and was regarded as a most fearful omen.

The fate of Cromwell's head

After death, Cromwell was first buried with great pomp in the tomb of the kings at Westminster, but after the Restoration his body was dug up and hung in the gibbet at Tyburn, with his head on a pole above Westminster Hall. The body was eventually buried quietly by the family, but the head stayed in place until it blew down in a thunderstorm twenty-five years later.

The head, it is said, was picked up by a sentry and taken home to be placed in his chimney corner. By the 1930s it was in the possession of a clergyman in Woodbridge, Suffolk, who bequeathed it to the Masters and Fellows of Sidney Sussex College, Cambridge (Cromwell's old college). They buried it in 1960 in an unmarked spot within the ante-chapel of the college.

It is noticeable that the only statue in Cambridgeshire of Cromwell is in St Ives, where he lived for just five years in the 1630s. A half-hearted attempt had been made in Huntingdon to raise funds for such a statue to celebrate the 300th anniversary of his birth, but it was left to the people of St Ives to commission and install the bronze sculpture, which was unveiled in 1901.

With regards to the locations of these seventeenth-century tales, Woodcroft Castle is in private hands. The Fleece at Southery still exists but is now known as The Old White Bell. The Bell in St Germain Street, Huntingdon was demolished in the 1990s.

The Brotherhood of the Grey Goose Feather is believed to have died out, and for a time, with the increased drainage, so too did the presence of the greylag goose in the East Anglian Fens. But whilst the greylag goose has been reintroduced in many areas of the UK, and numbers have increased significantly, the Brotherhood seems not to have survived or been revived.

For those who might be sceptical about the whole idea of the Brotherhood of the Grey Goose Feather, Gordon Phillips, who runs workshops to teach traditional Fenland Molly dancing to primary-school children may have found the proof. Phillips includes the telling of the grey goose feather story within his teaching sessions, and has been informed by two different children, one in Littleport and the other in Benwick, that they had found a grey goose feather amongst the possessions of their great-grandfathers after their death, but had, until then, no idea of the significance!

BIBLIOGRAPHY AND SOURCES

Bales, E.G. (1939) Folklore from West Norfolk, in *Folklore*, Vol. 50, No. 1, March

Banks, S.E. and Binns, J.W. (2002) *Gervase of Tilbury Otia Imperialia – Recreation for an Emperor* (Oxford: Clarendon Press)

Barrett, W.H. (1963) *Tales From the Fens* (London: Routledge & Kegan Paul)

Barrett, W.H. (1964) *More Tales from the Fens* (Routledge & Kegan Paul)

Bede, Cuthbert (1866) *Notes & Queries*, Third Series, Vol. 8, Vol. 9

Bevis, Trevor (1992) *Mini Stories from the Fens* (published by the author)

Bevis, Trevor (1995) *Hereward of the Fens – Incorporating Gesta Herewardi Saxonis* (published by the author)

Bigelow, M.M. (1881) *Placita Anglo-Normannica: Law Cases from William I to Richard I* [1066–1195] (Boston: Soule and Bugbee)

Booth, Steve (1997) Fenland Rebels, in *Green Anarchist*, Spring, Issue 45–46

Briggs, Katharine (1969) *A Dictionary of British Folk Tales – Folk Narratives* (London: Routledge & Kegan Paul)

Briggs, K.M. and Tongue, R.L. (1965) *Folktales of England* (London: Routledge & Kegan Paul)

Brown, Theo (1958) The Black Dog, in *Folklore*, Vol. 69, No. 3

Caporael, Linda R. (1976) Ergotism: The Satan Loosed in Salem?, in *Science*, 192, 2 April

Carter, Mary (1998) *Hemingford Grey is Famous for its Enormous Gooseberries; History Through Road Names* (Huntingdon: Westmeare Publishing)

Clare, John (1821) *The Village Minstrel and Other Poems* (Stamford: E. Drury)

Clare, John (1998) (ed. Eric Robinson) *John Clare: Poems of the Middle Period, 1822–1837* (Oxford: Oxford University Press)

Collier, J.P. (1841) *Robin Good-Fellow: His Mad Pranks and Merry Jests* [1628], reprinted for the Percy Society (London: C. Richards)

Conybeare, Edward (1897) *History of Cambridgeshire* (London: Elliot Stock)

Davenport, John (1646) *The Witches of Huntingdon 1646, Their Examinations and Confessions*, printed by W. Wilson for R. Clutterbuck

Day, Anthony (1988) Wicken's Lost Policeman, in *Cambridgeshire and Peterborough Life Magazine*, March

Day, James Wentworth (1954) *Here are Ghosts & Witches* (London: Batsford)

Day, James Wentworth (1973) *A History of the Fens* (London: George Harrap & Co.)

Day, James Wentworth (1954) *Ghosts and Witches – Haunted Tales from the British Isles* (London: Batsford)

Defoe, Daniel (1722) *Tour through the Eastern Counties of England* (Republished 1984 by *East Anglian Magazine Ltd*, Suffolk)

Drukker, T. (2003) Thirty-three Murderous Sisters: A Pre-Trojan Foundation Myth in the Middle English Prose *Brut* Chronicle, in *The Review of English Studies*, New Series, Vol. 54, No. 216, September

Ekirch, A. Roger (2005) *At Days Close: A History of Nighttime* (London: Weidenfeld & Nicolson)

Facetiae Cantabrigienses: consisting of anecdotes, smart sayings, satirics, retorts, etc., etc. by or relating to celebrated Cantabs, dedicated to the students of Lincoln's Inn' (1825)

Fairweather, Janet (ed.) (2005) *Liber Eliensis – A History of the Isle of Ely* (Woodbridge: Boydell & Brewer)

Fea, Allen (1907) *Nooks and Corners of Old England* (London: Eveleigh Nash)

Gaskill, M. (2005) *Witchfinders: A Seventeenth-Century English Tragedy* (London: John Murray)

Gerrard, V. (2003) *The Story of the Fens* (London: Robert Hale)

Goetinck, G. (1988) *The Wandlebury Legend and Welsh Romance*, Proceedings of the Cambridge Antiquarian Society, Vol. LXXVII

Gomme, G.L. (1885) *The History of Thomas Hickathrift* (London: Villon Society)

Gomme, G.L. (ed.) (1883) *The Gentleman's Magazine Library: Being a Classified Collection of the Chief Contents of the Gentleman's Magazine from 1731 to 1868*

Halliwell, J.O. (1970) *Popular Rhymes & Nursery Tales* (London: Bodley Head)

Halpert, H. and Thomas, G. (2001) Two Patterns of an International Tale: The Lawyer's Letter Opened, in *Fabula*, Vol. 42, Issue 1–2

Head, Victor (1995) *Hereward* (Stroud: Sutton Publishing)

Hone, William (1838) *The Every-Day Book and Table Book*, Vol. II (London: Thomas Tegg and Son)

Howat, Polly (1998) *Ghosts & Legends of Cambridgeshire* (Newbury: Countryside Books)

Hughes, T. McKenny and Hughes, Mary C. (1909) *Cambridgeshire: Cambridge County Geographies* (Cambridge: Cambridge University Press)

Ingoldsby, Thomas (1864) *Ingoldsby Legends or Mirth and Marvels* (London: Richard Bentley)

Johnson, C. (1893) *The Ely and Littleport Riots with an Account of the Trials and Executions in 1816* (Littleport: Harris)

Kingsley, Charles (1866) *Hereward the Wake* (London: Macmillan)

Lethbridge, T.C. (1957) *Gogmagog: The Buried Gods* (London: Routledge & Kegan Paul)

Lindley, Keith (1982) *Fenland Riots and the English Revolution* (London: Heinemann)

Lister, I.F. (1953) The Ordeal of Elizabeth Woodcock, in *The East Anglian Magazine*, Vol. 12

Lyon, Russell (2003) *The Quest for the Original Horse Whisperers* (Edinburgh: Luath Press Ltd)

Marlowe, Christopher (1926) *Legends of the Fenland People* (London: Cecil Palmer)

Meadows, P. and Ramsey, N. (2003) (ed.) *A History of Ely Cathedral* (Woodbridge: Boydell Press)

Miller, S.H. (1891) The Story of Bricstan of Chatteris, in W.H. Saunders (ed.) (1891) *Fenland notes & Queries*

Morris, Charles (1908) *Historical Tales: Scandinavian* (Los Angeles: Angelus University)

Murray, Tina (1992) A Victorian Melodrama in Three Acts, in *The Journal*, 3 December

Muskett, Paul (1984) Riotous Assemblies: Popular Disturbances in East Anglia 1740–1822 (Cambridgeshire: EARO)

Newman, L.F. (1945) Some Notes on the Folklore of Cambridgeshire and the Eastern Counties, in *Folklore*, Vol. 56, No. 3, September

Nichols, John Beverley (1934) *A Book of Old Ballads* (London: Hutchinson & Co.)

Noble, W.M. (1911) *Huntingdonshire: Cambridge County Geographies* (Cambridge: Cambridge University Press)

Notestein, Wallace (1911) *A History of Witchcraft in England from 1558 to 1718* (New York: American Historical Association)

Paddick, E.W. (1971) *Hoddesdon: Tales of a Hertfordshire Town* (Hoddesdon: Urban District Council)

Pattison, G.W. (1953) Adult Education and Folklore, in *Folklore*, Vol. 64, No. 3

Peacock, A.J. (1965) *Bread or Blood. A Study of the Agrarian Riots in East Anglia in 1816* (London: V. Gollancz)

Percy, Thomas (1906 reprint of 1765) *Reliques of Ancient English Poetry* (London: J.M. Dent)

Porter, E. (1969) *Cambridgeshire Customs & Folklore* (London: Routledge & Kegan Paul)

Porter, E. (1974) *Folklore of East Anglia* (London: Batsford)

Porter, Enid (ed.) (1975) *Victorian Cambridge – Josiah Chater's Diaries 1844–83* (London: Phillimore)

Pugh, R.B. (2002) The Liberty of Ely: Origins of the Liberty of Ely, in *A History of the County of Cambridge and the Isle of Ely: Volume 4: City of Ely; Ely, N. and S. Witchford and Wisbech Hundreds* (ed.) R. Pugh *et al.*

Randall, Arthur (1966) *Sixty Years a Fenman* (London: Routledge & Kegan Paul)

Saunders, John (1894) (ed.) *Chaucer's Canterbury Tales* (London: J.M. Dent & Co.)

Saunders, W.H. Bernard (1888) *Legends and Traditions of Huntingdonshire* (London: Simpkin, Marshall & Co.)

Saunders, W.H. Bernard (1891) *Fenland Notes & Queries*. A quarterly antiquarian journal for the Fenland, in the counties of Huntingdon, Cambridge, Lincoln, Northampton, Norfolk and Suffolk, Volume I (April 1889–October 1891)

Scott, Walter (1884) *Letters on Demonology and Witchcraft* (London: G. Routledge & Sons)

Sherb, V.I. (2002) Assimilating Giants: The Appropriation of Gog and Magog in Medieval and Early Modern England, in *Journal of Medieval and Early Modern Studies*, 32, Vol.1, Winter

Sherwood, Jones & Co. (1825) *The Terrific Register: Or, Record of Crimes, Judgments, Providences, and Calamities, Vol II* (London: Sherwood Jones & Co.)

Sneesby, N. (1999) *Etheldreda: Princess, Queen, Abbess & Saint* (Ely: Fern House)

Tatum, M. (1993) *The Witches of Warboys* (Cambridgeshire: Libraries Publications)

Tebbutt, C.F. (1984) *Huntingdonshire Folklore* (St Ives: Friends of the Norris Museum)

Thorpe, L. (trans.) (1976) *Geoffrey of Monmouth: The History of the Kings of Britain* (London: Penguin)

Walker J. (ed.) (1814) *A Selection of Curious Articles from the Gentleman's Magazine, Vol VI* (London: Gentleman's Magazine)

Warren, P (1997) *Report of the Trials for Rioting at Ely and Littleport 1816* (Cambridgeshire: Philip Warren)

Warren, W.L. (1966) *King John* (London: Penguin)

Waters, Richard (2003) *The Lost Treasure of King John* (Lincolnshire: Barny Books)

Williamson, Lindsay (1974) *Fen Folk: Tales from South Lincolnshire and the Cambridgeshire Fens* (Stamford: Spiegl Press)

Young, Francis (2013) *Witches and Witchcraft in Ely* (published by the author)

Archive sources

Eastern Counties Folklore Society archives in Cambridge University Library

Enid Porter notebooks at the Cambridge Folk Museum

Mason, K. (undated paper) The Murder of PC26 Richard Peak, Cambridgeshire Constabulary in the Cambridgeshire County Archives

Mossop, David (2000) Caxton Gibbet – notes in the Cambridgeshire Collection, Cambridge Central Library

Old Pygall's Story as told by Barrett at his bedside in Framingham Pigot, Norfolk, and broadcast on BBC Radio in July 1960, photocopy kindly provided by members of the family

Peckover, J. (1868) Transcript of a paper read by Jonathan Peckover at Wisbech Working Mens' Club and Institute, December 1868, in the Wisbech & Fenland Museum

Picton, M. (1972) The Hereward Legends – Unpublished PhD thesis, available on the British Library electronic database

Online sources

www.friendsofnormancross.org.uk
www.greatfen.org.uk
www.hiddenea.com
www.marshlandstjames.com
www.welney.org.uk

About the Author

MAUREEN JAMES is an historian, writer, storyteller and teacher. She gained a passion for history as a result of reading an historical novel in 1985, and has since devoted much of her time to researching and spreading this passion by whatever means possible. Her education has since included undergraduate studies at Cambridge University, a Masters Degree at the University of London and, in 2013, she was awarded the title Doctor of Philosophy for her research into the legends of the Carrs, which included work on the folklore, folk tales and storytellers of Cambridgeshire. The spread of her love of the past has included museum education, living history presentations, talks, lectures and writing. She is also a regular contributor to *Smallholder Magazine* on the subject of history, folklore and folk customs. Maureen has found, however, that the most effective way to share her passion for things historical has been through the medium of the spoken voice, particularly telling historical stories that are evocative of mood, place and time. She often wears historical costume and has told her stories – which are particularly from Cambridgeshire, though her repertoire now includes many other British stories – at diverse venues including medieval manor houses, iron-age forts, castles and abbeys, and even in a barn standing beside a lively Exmoor pony. More recently she has regularly been seen dressed as a Victorian folklorist spreading her knowledge of folklore and folk tales at summer events. For further information see her website www.tellinghistory.com.

If you enjoyed this book, you may also be interested in …

Lincolnshire Folk Tales

MAUREEN JAMES

Lincolnshire's folk tales still resonate within the rural landscape. From the dark tales of the 'Buried Moon' and the 'Werewolf of Langrick Fen', to the humorous tales of 'The Lad that went to look for Fools' and the 'Farmer and the Boggart', these tales take us back to a time when the people would huddle around the fire in the mud and stud cottages to while away the long winter evenings.

978 0 7524 6640 8

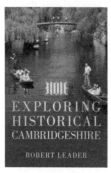

Exploring Historical Cambridgeshire

ROBERT LEADER

This beautifully photographed guidebook follows Cambridgeshire's waterways: from leafy Huntingdon to the wide-sky Fens, along the Nene Valley down to Wisbech and besides the gentle stream of the Cam. From the bizarre Straw Bears that lead the hosts of morris dancers through the heart of Whittlesey, to the sedate Rose Fair that graces Wisbech church, Cambridgeshire has something to offer everyone.

978 0 7509 6032 8

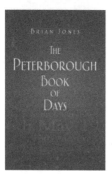

The Peterborough Book of Days

BRIAN JONES

A day-by-day guide to Peterborough's history, this book contains political, sporting, criminal, strange, amusing and eccentric events from different periods in the history of the cathedral city. Some events had a major impact on the history of the country as a whole, whilst others are just plain absurd!

978 0 7524 7932 3

Visit our website and discover thousands of other History Press books.

www.thehistorypress.co.uk